HEAVEN'S DYNAMITE

HEAVEN'S DYNAMITE

God's Amazing Power to Heal the Sick

Mike Endicott

Terra Nova Publications

Published in Great Britain by
Terra Nova Publications Ltd
PO Box 2400, Bradford on Avon, Wiltshire BA15 2YN

Scripture quotations taken from the
Holy Bible, New International Version.
Copyright © 1973, 1978, 1984 by International Bible Society.
Used by permission of Hodder and Stoughton Ltd.
All rights reserved.

ISBN 1 90194 921 4

Printed in Great Britain by
Bookmarque Ltd, Croydon, Surrey

Contents

FOREWORD

The Revd. Dr. Russ Parker

There is a new wind of expectancy blowing through the world of Christian healing and it is one of anticipation that God wants to give us a profound experience of his ability to powerfully heal those with physical diseases. The question is not so much, 'Will God do it?' but, 'Are we ready to see it happen amongst us?'

Naturally there are dangers, such as people being made to feel inferior because they did not receive the cure they were expecting. Horror stories abound of people being told that their faith was faulty in some way or that there was some spiritual blockage in their family background. This wrongly suggests that God's power to heal is limited.

The opposite mistake is to be so uncomfortable with miracles and power that we reduce Christian healing to little more than comforting the sick with good hope of endurance and the promise of eternity where all our sicknesses will cease. In so doing we reduce Jesus to a passive carer, rather than the Son of God who heals the sick and casts out demons.

To be true to our calling we must be open to the mighty acts of God's power to heal every sickness, as well as being ready to live with sometimes not seeing the healing we so much want. This is the life of risky faith, which Mike Endicott calls us to embrace, and in so doing, to follow Jesus on the adventure of healing power. Mike's book offers wonderful stories of healing, and good teaching to inspire us to get up and go and do what Jesus did.

Introduction

A lady who had never before asked for prayer was clutching her Zimmer frame. She stood on the line of silver tape along the carpet that serves as an altar rail at The Well Centre, a place of Christian healing in Cwmbran, South Wales. A time of teaching—on the subject of our need to expect the miraculous—was coming to an end, and a queue of people was forming on the healing line. There was a great sense of expectancy. Keeping both hands tightly on the frame, she said, "I've had three major back operations but I am still left in considerable pain. I can only walk a few steps with my frame and then I have to sit down, as the pain gets too strong for me. Will you pray about my pain?" Within fifteen minutes she had walked two laps around the big room at The Well, and had set out on her third trip, followed by one of the ministry team who was carrying the Zimmer behind her! By the end of the evening she was free of all pain and singing at the top of her voice.

A few weeks earlier, another crippled lady had been leaning on her front doorpost, propped up by her crutches, enjoying the early summer sunshine. Extreme back pain had stolen her livelihood, and despair at a bleak and painful future had overcome her. A friend who happened to be walking by on the way to the village shop stopped to commiserate with her. The ensuing conversation might have seemed to most people to be naïve, and bordering on the unreal:

"Would you like Jesus to heal your back?"

"I don't think he would. I'm not one of you Christians, you know!"

"Ring this number and ask the Christians there to pray with you —nothing ventured, nothing gained!" A week later, to the astonishment of her family, friends, employer and doctor, she was back at work, completely restored.

Stories like these are not so unusual in the church today. There was a time when such things, whilst greeted with much joy when they occurred, were rarely seen. But the times have changed. It is not just that God has issued some fresh anointing on a few individuals to perform miracles for him, but that the anointing to heal the sick has always resided in the church, and that a fresh revelation of scriptural truth is releasing keys to unlock God's grace and power. We have been given some simple keys to releasing healing, which lead us to expect a considerable number of such miracles at every meeting. These are exciting days!

Men and women who have carried the healing, saving gospel to Africa, South America and India record with an obvious thrill how hundreds have simply and openly received the healing grace of God. All somehow agree that it is so much easier 'out there'. A number of reasons have been suggested for that apparent imbalance in the flow of God's acts of miraculous healing around the world. It is often pointed out that societies have different cultural and educational traditions: very different attitudes to the scientific world view, and so on. The fact is that many churches in the non-Western world have a wonderful spirit of simple acceptance of biblical truth, whilst the European churches, in so many instances, have become filled with scepticism. Wherever we see God at work in miraculous power, we also see a childlike, simple, trusting expectancy into which the river of grace can flow. This is not for one moment to suggest that Christian healing is opposed to the scientific, medical understanding of illness. Simple, expectant, trusting faith in the supernatural power of God is not anti-intellectual.

Revivals have been marked by **expectancy** —and the receiving of miracles, especially miracles of healing. When a meeting can take place between our expectancy and divine grace, it is as though heaven 'explodes'. We might say that 'grace plus expectancy' triggers heaven's dynamite, because when real, expectant trust is there, and God is moving amongst his people, his power begins to flow. We begin to see sick people healed. Put like that, it sounds rather like a description of a chemical reaction. But we must not make the mistake of thinking in a *mechanistic* way about divine, supernatural power. God's love is always personal; his dealings with us are relational, and the initiative is his, for he has reached out to us, giving himself for us. God wants his people to live in expectant, trusting faith, and he uses that faith; we must always remember that he is the one who has led us to that position of faith. His grace comes first. Nor are we to see human action as the cause or source of what God releases. That would be a serious error. The word 'grace' preserves us from such a misunderstanding. 'Grace' means free gift — it is the right word to describe all that Jesus has done for us. When we speak of divine grace, we are acknowledging that faith (and expectant trust for healing), like all good things, is the gift of our loving heavenly Father God—not something *we* generate.

In our bodies we have many mechanisms for natural healing, and that is how God intended it to be. The created order is *his* creation, though marred by man's disobedience and 'enemy activity'. What we might categorise as 'natural' or 'supernatural', in God's economy are not as distinct as we might think, for he is Lord over all —the 'natural' world and those special events that we call miracles.

God's power, like his love, is infinite. When we read in the Gospels of the many miracles Jesus did, we see divine power at work. In all those familiar Gospel accounts we see what trusting expectancy toward the Father, in the power of the Holy Spirit, looks like; and we see, too, that the relationship between Jesus and the Father means that all things are possible with God.

Is it that simple? Could God really have made the healing of the sick as easy as it seems to have been in the New Testament? In this book I will show that the answer is an emphatic *yes*. The problem is that we too often want to make it so much more complicated. Scepticism—unbelief—has all too often made the healing ministry of the Christian church into a hit-and-miss 'religious' affair, trying it now and again to see if God will 'do the business'.

Our requests may sometimes be hopeful, but are much less often marked by real, confident, trusting **expectancy**. What we call the ministry of healing is often a kind of ministry of praying (by which I mean intercession in the presence of the supplicant), but less often a place where God's work gets visibly done. But there is incomparably great power available to us who believe, who are God's 'new creation'. We Christians have all been given the awesome and exciting responsibility of carrying the revealed word of God, together with the signs and wonders accompanying that word, to the world. Every church, of course, prays for those who are sick in various ways, but perhaps more out of Christian hope, love and duty than the real expectation that God will act, according to his promises. Add in the particular ingredient **expectancy**, add **persistence** and **humility**, and those around the church begin to be healed of their sicknesses in numbers perhaps only dreamed of before.

This book has been written to describe our re-discovery of the truth of God's word during the first year of a longed-for move of the Holy Spirit, and so to encourage others to learn what is needed to serve more effectively in the precious ministry of Christian healing.

I keep asking that the God of our Lord Jesus Christ, the glorious Father, may give you the Spirit of wisdom and revelation, so that you may know him better.

I pray also that the eyes of your heart may be enlightened in order that you may know the hope to which he has called you, the riches of his glorious inheritance in the saints, and his incomparably great power for us who believe. That power is like the working of his mighty strength, which he exerted in Christ when he raised him from the dead and seated him at his right hand in the heavenly realms, far above all rule and authority, power and dominion, and every title that can be given, not only in the present age but also in the one to come. And God placed all things under his feet and appointed him to be head over everything for the church, which is his body, the fullness of him who fills everything in every way.

Ephesians 1:17–23

1

Walking into the Miraculous

Those who have been healed by Jesus have wonderful, true stories to tell of his amazing power and love at work in their lives today. Here is just a small selection of the thrilling testimonies we have been sent, from those who have received the healing touch of Jesus.

Dear All,

Some years ago I injured my back as a result of being thrown across the cabin of an offshore boat I was skippering during a gale off the Thames Estuary. About a year later I had an MRI scan, which showed that as part of the body's natural healing process, excess bone material had flowed into my spine to mend it and had clamped around the spinal cord. This made it very painful to do much. I saw a specialist privately, who said that he could operate to remove the excess bone, and offered to operate the following week for approximately £5,000. Alternatively, on the NHS waiting list, the operation would be deferred for at least a year. I could not afford the £5,000 and became certain in my own mind that the Lord would heal my back. After five days of much prayer, I awoke one morning and jumped out of bed ready to take the dog for a walk in the woods. Then I realised that there was no pain, and that the Lord had healed me! That was the first of several physical healings. The second came when a car door was slammed on my thumb. It was quite badly crushed, split most of the way round and the bone broken in several places. I knelt at the communion rail one morning, at the church where I am churchwarden, took the splint off my thumb and held it up to the Lord. all crushed and broken and stitched up. I compared my two thumbs and asked him that in his mercy he would heal my (left) thumb. Needless to say, I am now looking at my two thumbs and they are both perfect; only the very faintest of marks shows where all the bits joined up —and I have to look very closely to see even that! So God has been very good. And this brings me to the recent healing day at The Well Centre. Last July, I had twisted my ankle quite badly whilst in the woods. Eventually, I had an x-ray which showed bits of bone splinters and cracks in the bone, together with damage to the ligaments. Again, I have gone to a specialist and have now had an MRI scan. I am awaiting an appointment with the specialist to hear what the results of the scan are and to see the scan pictures.

My recent visit to The Well Centre was something of a bonus. During the afternoon session, the team kindly offered to pray for healing for my ankle. One of them reported a great heat coming off my ankle, and I knew that the Lord was doing something. When I got up, I found that the pain was gone from my ankle. I was able to confirm to the others the nature of the problem and that all pain seemed to have disappeared, but could not say anything more. I felt that I would liked to have said, "Hurrah, I am healed!" —but it seems very important to be precise in public and not to exceed the horizon of one's knowledge. I am now living in a state of permanent excitement at the way in which the Lord is using me —particularly, it seems, to bring an awareness of the work of the Holy Spirit to (what was) a very conventional and conservative parish. It all seems to have sprung from my studies of the modules which you prepared for those wishing to enter the healing ministry. Thank you again for all that you are doing. Hope that the Lord blesses you richly — thank you for helping me to come more closely into his presence.

David

Dear Mike,

Here is an account of my healing from sciatica, which I had suffered down my left leg for a long time. My vicar had prayed for healing from it; it did improve, but returned after a short while. At a conference last year, you asked anyone to come forward who had received healing before but their condition had returned. As I stood there you prayed, and immediately the pain vanished. You emphasised that if the condition returned, we each must immediately tell it to go, as we had been healed. Over the next few weeks, whenever I felt it returning I bade it go in Jesus name as I had been healed. It did, and soon gave up trying! Alleluia! I am constantly wanting to praise and thank him, I want others to experience what I have; my prayers for others have new impetus and I want people to really believe in God's healing grace. As for me, I constantly rejoice in freedom from pain.

Pauline

Hello Mike!

Just a quick note to praise God with you that I am free of migraines at last. I have had one of those terrible things every week for twelve years which, as you can imagine, was totally draining. It's now three months since one occurred and life is really flooding back into all my veins. Hallelujah!

Madeline

Dear Mike,

At one of your training weekends on healing, the Lord fulfilled his promise to heal me completely from a stroke, which struck me down in January 1998. As I was recovering in hospital, the doctors told me I can look forward to 50% mobility after the total paralysis down my left side. God then spoke to me and said that 50% plus him made for 100% healing. This was a promise I held on to for the next four years. We had had lectures and been writing quite intensely over the Friday night and Saturday. That evening, we had a service of blessing. Three of the ministry team came to me, covered me with a representation of the robe of righteousness, anointed me with oil and prayed for me. I was told to stay kneeling and they came back a further three times to pray with me. I told the Lord I could not stay in this position for more than two minutes as the pain becomes so intense. He only told me to rest. I remember hearing the others praying twice more. I had been there for 45 minutes.

When I awoke on Sunday morning I felt so well and strong. By habit I picked up my walking stick to go to breakfast, but found it irritated me and got in the way. So I put it down again and walked upright into the dining room. I felt so good and knew the Lord had done something, but it was only at lunch that I realised how much. Due to lack of grip in my left hand, I needed my food cut up, as I could not hold a fork. I sat down at the table and without thinking picked up my knife and fork and started cutting up my meal. I then realised my left shoulder which was out of joint, preventing full movement was the same as my right shoulder, in its proper place. After further investigation, I found that the lumps of wasted muscle in my arm and behind my knee had disappeared and my limbs were normal. I then started praising God for completing his promise to heal me 100% from the stroke. Since then I have been enjoying travelling around without a stick, driving an ordinary gear-change car, and able to be—as one or two people have commented—normal once again. One of my daughters, with tears in her eyes, commented that I looked better than I have done for years. I am praising God for his love and faithfulness to his word, even personal words to each of us.

Maureen

Dear Mike,

Almost a week has passed, and I have not written to thank you for an amazing experience last Sunday. I admit that my original intention was to go to a Taizé worship evening, but when a friend asked us whether we could give her a lift to your service in the local town, both my wife and I leapt at the chance. Of course, the Lord was working through her, because he wanted us to be with you, and I have been giving heartfelt thanks all the week. We have all been brainwashed into thinking in an entirely materialistic way. 'Healing like that is unscientific— much better to go to a proper doctor!' (I have heard so often). So we all tend to become cynics, but you shattered my inbuilt cynicism in one evening—I hope permanently. I am afraid we all talk too much and put it into practice too little, e.g. we all cheer-fully say that we can lay our burden on the Lord, but we don't do it, and you showed us what it means. Last Sunday, we saw REAL prayer, and it re-ally can move mountains. Blessings.

Charles

...I would like to take a moment out of today to thank you, The Well Centre team, and to glorify God for his goodness, grace and limitless love. Last week impacted so much change on my life it is truly difficult to know where to begin. I can join the 'happy clappy' with the best of them; but there is no depth to it for me personally. I have learned that our own individual experience of Jesus is different; he meets us all as individual people and the respect he gives us in that role is unique to our own circumstance, experience and future. Last week, I stood at the beginning again. As you spoke of God healing, my head knew it; my mind had read it in a great many books; but I had never personally experienced it. The 'Thomas' in my nature revealed itself. I, too, wanted to put my finger in the holes in his hands. The burning desire in me was to experience more than just a reading experience. God was gracious. There was a healing in me needed that I did not even know existed.... As I watched your confidence in God being displayed, I found it to be infectious and contagious. I met the Jesus of the New Testament, not just before my eyes in the many healings I witnessed, but in my mind, my heart and soul. Healing for me personally came in the removal of my doubts, my insecurities and lack of expectation. My battle for understanding was removed, and I learned to accept that God is God. There were many healings on site last week, some for us all to see, but others were internal and those will be displayed in the working out of our daily lives. Have I come home with my head in the clouds? Not at all, in fact my feet have never been firmer on the ground than they are now. I met with the living Jesus. I saw. I heard. I touched. I smelt. And, finally, I now know the living God.

Helen

Jean's story (71 when she wrote this.)

Dear everybody in the office,

I was getting ready to go on the Away Day at Weston–super–Mare for the *Alpha* course when I fell and broke my arm.   This resulted in my attending hospital to have my arm set. Because of my emphysema, I was unable to have anaesthetic so had to have my arm set unaided, which was very painful. I was in agony of pain. I had a terrible night, and on Sunday the pain was awful —so bad that I went back to the hospital, and was told I might have to have an operation, which would be very risky.   In the evening I went with May, my neighbour, to Zion Baptist Church, where a service of healing was to take place. After the preacher, Rev. Mike Endicott, who was blind, had spoken, we were invited to go out to the front, where a team from Jacob's Well Ministries prayed with me and asked for the pain to go away and that I would not have to have an operation. The pain subsided as they prayed, and by the time I got home it had gone away altogether and I had a wonderful night's sleep. I feel God took away my pain, and thank him for that, and the team for their prayers. Next morning, I returned to the hospital and they didn't have to operate —isn't God good? I go back tomorrow and am trusting God for further healing!

Those are only a few of the letters we have received, but can it be like this for all of us? Can any one of us walk forward from wherever we are into the miraculous life? Can we all receive healing? Can all believers be used as 'channels' in this glorious kingdom work?

The theme of this book is quite simply that if we learn to *expect* God to be faithful to his promises we shall see more and more of the abundant life which Jesus came to bring —and that includes healing!

2

A Crisis of Confidence

Why, we may wonder in this modern and scientific age, should God be interested in resurrecting the ministry of the healing of the sick? A simple answer may be that, of all his gracious gifts to the world, nothing so undeniably demonstrates his presence among us than divinely recreated wholeness. And how much the world needs this witness! There exists, without doubt, a vast and widening chasm between the life of the local church and the thousands of people who live in the parish area. Most of them have bypassed and sidelined the church as being totally irrelevant; most will only be vaguely aware of its location. At worst they are not interested, they do not know it exists, nor do they want to know.

In the face of such crushing apathy, and with the burden of falling numbers and finances, the church thrashes around in search of any mission straw to help keep her afloat. We test out new styles of worship services and drive our congregations ever onwards into outreach programmes of every description, secretly hoping that such efforts will all eventually be rewarded by increasing congregations. When such projects fail, we defend our lack of success by claiming that numbers are not important anyway. The difficulty here is that God thinks they are! So what about mission in the local church? Are we going about it in the right way? The place to start must surely be the apostolic pattern for mission which can clearly be seen in the first letter to Timothy.

> I urge, then, first of all, that requests, prayers, intercession and thanksgiving be made for everyone—for kings and all those in authority, that we may live peaceful and quiet lives in all godliness and holiness. This is good, and pleases God our Saviour, who wants all men to be saved and to come to a knowledge of the truth. For there is one God and one mediator between God and men, the man Christ Jesus, who gave himself as a ransom for all men—the testimony given in its proper time. And for this purpose I was appointed a herald and an apostle—I am telling the truth, I am not lying—and a teacher of the true faith to the Gentiles.
>
> *I Timothy 2:1–7*

Timothy was given a somewhat tough assignment — he was set aside to supervise the churches in the regions of Ephesus. His remit was to proclaim the gospel positively; to correct the damage that seems to have been done before his arrival by false teachers; and to lay down patterns of proper congregational life. Paul is giving directions to Timothy concerning public worship, and he is emphasising that a congregation's first priority is to be a worshipping and a praying community. This is where everything begins: our first priority must be Godward. Having this as our priority prepares us to be more effective in our reaching out to others, and changes us into God-centred people —and the sort of people we are witnesses to our beliefs. Yet, in reality, we church folk can so often behave more like noisy, clashing children on the school playground than mature Christians. Will they know we are Christians by our love? Perhaps not, after some of those more convoluted and argumentative committee discussions about the use of the parish hall kitchen, or the motion on the agenda to hold a joint service with that other denomination down the road. It is here, unhappily, in the local bearpit of our church community, that we display to any passing onlooker our priorities and our attitudes. A controlling priest, a churchwarden looking to cement his rank and position, or a choir clique, can all undermine witness and outreach. Onlookers casually observe the way we go about things, and sometimes perceive a huge difference between what we say or sing and what we *do*. But a church of mature, loving and Christ-filled hearts can bring amazing healing to broken lives.

In I Timothy 2 we are told, firstly, that a church should be ***praying***. We need to pray daily for key leaders in our community —that they might know the will of God, and that he might govern them. But that is just the beginning. Paul is urging that the church is to pray for ***everyone***, and this is our top priority. Prayer is absolutely fundamental to reaching people. God wants all to be saved, and Jesus died for all. We must never lose our sense of awe at the wonder and the magnificence of the gospel: that God's love should be manifested in such an amazing way —that the divine Son of God should come and die in our place. Secondly, Christians are to witness to all people. Paul writes that he has been appointed as a herald, an apostle, and a teacher to all nations. That is the apostolic pattern, and we need to imitate it. The church is to be a powerhouse, from which mission emerges, rather than a toothless, sleeping lion, waving the tip of her frustrated tail from time to time at any passing fly of secularism. In God's economy, a central place in mission has been assigned to the local church as the base camp for outreach. To make this a reality we need to pay attention to three aspects of our congregational life. Firstly, minister and people need to ensure that their lives are on track in terms of godliness and holiness of living. Unless our lives are fundamentally consistent with biblical truths, all our outreach will lead to despair, and will be hollow and empty. The very people with whom we seek to share our faith will see right through us. Secondly, we in the congregations should get our home life on track. A stable Christian home has a mighty power for the gospel in a world weighed down with bent, broken and dysfunctional ones. Thirdly, a congregation needs to be on the same forgiving, accepting path that Jesus walked. It is useless to go out in outreach and bring people into an emotional refrigerator, where there is judgement, condemnation, bickering and division. A congregation has to be warm and welcoming, caring and loving; accepting each other with compassion, joy and enthusiasm. Jesus mixed with sinners; he did not shun their company, but ate with them as he ministered to them. Should not our congregation become a friendship centre? The evangelistic impact of a warm, loving, accepting and welcoming congregation can be tremendous. This is the arena where the love of God can be seen by anyone whose eyes are open.

> No one has ever seen God; but if we love one another, God lives in us and his love is made complete in us.
>
> *1 John 4:12*

God's present, continuous activity includes loving, encouraging, restoring and healing others through us — and that becomes an obvious demonstration of his power.

When we begin to understand this, there arises the question of knowing to whom we must go and minister. Let us travel together on an imaginary walk down the nearest street — the one outside your own front door will suffice perfectly — and interview every household, asking them to tell us about the problems that really touch their lives where it hurts. We could take with us three big cardboard boxes in which to put all the answers —and we would need to label them (not necessarily in order) 'money matters', 'relationship problems' and 'health'. Every opened front door would yield something for us. We might also need a pocketful of empty matchboxes for all the other little family niggles, but the big boxes would probably cover most of what we would hear. It would seem too obvious to state that any missionary congregation needs to know how the gospel touches on these key areas that are at the heart of people's concerns, yet we so often fail to see the connection. The Spirit of God within us would spur us, on opening those boxes, to pour God's love into each household —through caring, listening and offering Christian comfort, advice and, above all, the word of God, and the invitation to respond to Jesus.

Unhappily, though, the public image we have to live with is that of irrelevance. The 'old wineskin' of our religious routine is often perceived as being empty. At the same time, the exciting, positive thing is that many Christians have once more begun to discover the fatherhood of God. Fatherhood is an essential part of family life which is largely missing in the lives of many. The flow of acts of healing is to be understood as manifesting true fatherhood —demonstrations of a father's desire to see his children in a love relationship with him again, encouraged and strengthened in him. To listen carefully and diligently to the pain of the street is to hear a deep voice, further back in the depths of our very humanity —a deeply frustrated groan that cries out for real change. God places in people that yearning for himself. But hungry sheep look up expectantly to the pulpit and are not fed in these matters of reality. Starved of the living bread, we grow few in number, thin and sickly. Our response to God drifts relentlessly downhill from expectancy to a kind of wistful hoping that is less than true hope; and from that to despair. Is there nothing, we may ask, that Christianity can do for spiritually needy people? All too often we are fed not with the word of God but philosophy, theoretical allusion and clever intellectual analysis. So many carefully crafted sermons—mostly forgotten as soon as they are heard—lack power. Deism and multi-faith are becoming commonly accepted. Forms of religion with no power or substance are all too often offered in our churches. Preachers need not so much to cultivate erudition and the rhetorical arts, but to preach the cross of Jesus Christ, and the fatherhood of God —and so feed our hungry hearts.

The chasm between church and society has grown almost too wide to see across, and yet Jesus wants to save everybody. We really need to stand on the truth of the gospel: that Jesus Christ, the Son of the living God, died for our sins, according to the Scriptures, was buried, was raised from the dead on the third day, and appeared to many after his death and resurrection. (See 1 Corinthians 15:3f.) We need to teach positively that we cannot *earn* our position — the Father sent the Son to make us a new creation in him. Jesus came from the Father and returned to him. When we see Jesus, we see the Father. When we know the heart of Jesus, we know the heart of the Father. This is the powerful truth that changes lives, reconciling us to our heavenly Father, and it is all a free gift, appropriated through faith.

The people whom Jesus has come to save consist of body, mind and spirit; and the fact that our Father God heals the sick simply cannot be ignored. In our ministry, and in so many other biblically based ministries, we see it happen over and over again. It is extremely urgent that we should speak, preach and teach the *whole* truth about the living gospel that changes lives —or our nation will drift ever further to the false gods of this world. The healing good news must be preached; and the gifts of the Holy Spirit, too rarely seen in so many of our churches, are desperately needed. Medical science helps many people and can be a huge blessing, but neither it nor other human skills can adequately replace the extraordinary, supernatural healing activity of God. He has not withdrawn his hand in such matters. Historically, awareness of and openness to the amazing gifts of the Holy Spirit diminished in the church because so many Christians lost their love for Jesus, became lukewarm and were left with a dead form of religion in place of true joy, love and the pure, anointed word of God. Sadly, many churchgoers have lost all sense of excitement and delight in our amazing, life-transforming heavenly Father. Yet Jesus Christ came into the world to save sinners, and the role of our churches is to worship the Saviour and witness to this truth.

As well as growing ignorance of the truth of the word of God, one of the chief reasons why Christians have ceased to speak the gospel boldly to the community is fear of what the reaction to this message will be. When we adopt a biblical stance on some issue or other, we fail to explain our attitude as being an application of the word of God. We may fall into the trap of justifying our moral standpoints by some secular theory of ethics; and when our hurts, wounds and sicknesses are healed by Jesus we keep very quiet about it all. The most truly alarming aspect of all this is that we are not alarmed. We drift into accepting the secular world view that we have nothing of any importance to offer. We dare not be the salt that has lost its saltiness.

Let us be humble enough to allow our eyes to be opened to the wonder of our salvation! Healing miracles among the people will not automatically open the floodgates of revival, despite the evidence that many people today are crying out for a faith that works. But healing does accompany authentic preaching of the word: that is clearly demonstrated throughout the New Testament, and God has not changed. His will is to heal and to save.

> Yet at the same time many even among the leaders believed in him. But because of the Pharisees they would not confess their faith for fear they would be put out of the synagogue; for they loved praise from men more than praise from God.
>
> *John 12:42–43*

'If only Jesus would appear here, now, and do a miracle, I'd believe in him!' must be a common enough heartfelt thought among the unchurched in times of trial, but may have much less hope and truth in it than we might like to think. After three years of seeing miraculous signs and wonders, many of Jesus' contemporaries refused to believe. All the evidence in the world will not make us believers if we refuse to surrender our wills to the Lord: the life that is not surrendered to Jesus Christ remains in spiritual blindness, walking in the way of death rather than life. Those who persist in their rejection of Christ as saviour, healer and friend become increasingly hardened. The unbelieving mind becomes a closed one. Many are unwilling to receive the salvation he brings. He has come as a healer and restorer, but many do not want to be healed by him, and nor do they have any idea that they are walking in a darkness from which they need to be restored to the perfect relationship with himself that God intended. Healing is not merely the result of some wistful, half-meant prayer; we need to open a door to let Christ in.

To some extent, most of us draw a thick line between the sacred and the secular, perhaps intending to protect the sacred from pollution. That line which we draw also prevents the sacred from invading the 'secular' parts of our lives. Too many churchgoers think church and Christianity are for Sundays —that they are not 'real life'. So we keep our illnesses to ourselves, and regard our family business as our own. A stiff upper lip has become something of which to be proud. Compounding the mistake, we have often put other sorts of walls around our painful feelings from earlier days, and buried them well below the conscious level of the mind. We do this so that we will not have to feel or face them. I am not advocating excessive 'delving', least of all into wounds which have been healed and sins for which we have repented, but the problem is that when we put walls around painful, negative feelings we are still experiencing at some level, the same walls may go around our positive, warm, loving empathy as well. That is one reason why some reach the point of being dead, dry and empty inside —both towards the healing kingdom of our Father God, and towards the world outside it. Hardened, insensitive, cold, dry, dying hearts desperately need the life of our risen, living Lord Jesus.

The church bears some responsibility for society's lack of interest in the gospel, and its fascination with healing crystals, fortune telling and tarot card readings, because we have signally failed both to present a living, working faith, and to offer effective prayer for issues that really matter to people—including healing. Healing was never an optional extra in the early church, and although it has often been a neglected area of ministry, it has never been lost completely. As a witness to God's glory, the healing ministry is for all: the complete outsider, people on the fringes of the church, people in the pews who are seeking Jesus but have not yet had their eyes opened, and for church leaders, alike. It is absolutely central to the whole matter of mission and evangelism, if we are to see increasingly secularised societies re-conquered by the redemptive gospel of Jesus Christ. God wants to heal everyone; God wants to heal you!

3

The Hope of the Harvest

Healing is such an exciting ministry to be involved in. We learn from the Bible and from our present experience that God does wonderful things, moving in a supernatural way to transform situations. Jesus' priority was to proclaim the kingdom, according to the Father's will, as he was led by the Holy Spirit, and healing was a sign of that —the outworking of love, which resulted in changed lives. If we are to live as disciples of Jesus, then we have to follow his model, and healing—important as it is—was not and is not the absolute priority. The top priority is always worship, and prayer.

Wonderfully, wherever we turn, there is Jesus. He is the beginning, middle and end of everything to us. He is everything good, everything holy, all-beautiful and everything joyous to his servants. No one needs to be poor if he can have the friendship of Jesus. No one needs to be overly downcast, because Jesus Christ is the joy of heaven, and it is joyful to him to enter into hearts full of sorrow. There are many things that we can exaggerate about, but not the compassionate abundance of the love and the works of Jesus in us. We might talk about the grace of Jesus for the whole of a lifetime, but we would never come to the end of the precious things that might be said of him. With Jesus there is always a true hope, even in times of decline. He is the only source of new life for every generation, for he is King of kings and Lord of lords; his love is unchanging, his kingdom will never end. The Father has placed all judgement in his hands; he is the mighty Saviour of all who draw near to him and call upon his name.

This good news must be expressed with clarity and confidence. Miracles, divine intervention and social care have to go hand in hand with the proclamation of the gospel message, expressing the fullness of God's revelation of his nature, his invitation and his self-giving love. We sometimes hear of 'mission' defined as 'being Christ in the community'. How beguilingly smooth and comfortable that can sound. But consider the uncomfortable question: 'who is this Jesus Christ?' Is he just 'nice' or is he mighty, powerful, the only way, truth and life? In other words, is he who he said he is? Yes; we are to be kind to others; that sounds mild, perhaps, but what does 'kindness' mean to the Christian? It is an act of supernatural power and love. Peter described the healing of a crippled man as an 'act of kindness'.

If we are being called to account today for an act of kindness shown to a cripple and are asked how he was healed, then know this, you and all the people of Israel: It is by the name of Jesus Christ of Nazareth, whom you crucified but whom God raised from the dead, that this man stands before you healed.

Acts 4:9,10

In today's culture, such powerful 'acts of kindness'—healing, whether physical or emotional—sometimes lead people to a personal relationship with Jesus Christ. Our preaching of atonement will always lack an important dimension if we ignore healing, so amply demonstrated in the earthly ministry of Jesus and the witness of the whole of the New Testament. Our first and main task as Christians is to preach and witness to Jesus Christ crucified for our sins and alive now. Often, healing accompanies this authentic proclamation, because it remains true that, 'by his wounds we are healed' (Isaiah 53:5b) and we need to proclaim that word and teach Christians to claim it for themselves and others. The apostles ministered, as we do, in a multi-spiritual-choice culture, where truth claims competed for attention. In such a challenging environment they were not afraid to put themselves in the firing line, and to express complete confidence in the power of God to heal, save and deliver as they preached the cross. Today, as then, everyone needs to experience the supernatural power of God.

How is it that, in the thinking of so many churchgoers, our supremely powerful God has become 'boxed in, labelled and put away' somewhere up near the altar in church, where he is not expected to do anything unplanned? If we allow our past, present and future to be held in the redemptive, healing hands of the living Lord Jesus Christ, he really does move with extraordinary effect. So why is the *power* of God the most underused 'resource' in the church today? Possibly the greatest potential mission field is all around us, with pierced and tattooed bodies, drug abused brains, attitudes distorted by personal greed, media abused minds or emotionally broken hearts and disease shattered bodies. There are many folk waiting at the margins of church life. They sometimes look wistfully at our church buildings, wondering if they would be welcomed without being made to change from their natural ways into the uniform of some unusual ritual, or simply left feeling guilty and out of place. The church needs to be aware that the precious word of God, believed and spoken under the anointing of the Holy Spirit really can transform the ordinary daily lives of seekers. The most treasured and invaluable pearl of the human soul is hidden in the fallow ground of these wondering, wandering hearts, waiting for the fatherly plough of healing love to be brought to them with the mercy, gentleness and grace of Jesus Christ.

There are so many people who long to be enfolded and not discarded. If we have truly had a personal encounter with the living Lord Jesus, we know how wonderful he is. We discover that relationship to be the most important thing in life, but too many of us compartmentalise 'sacred' and 'secular'. There is no such division, because when we receive Jesus he comes and dwells within us. His light begins to shine in us, and we are to become 'transparent' to that light by being filled with the Holy Spirit, and engaging in spiritual warfare against the world, the flesh and the devil. Then Jesus is always with us, his power is at work within us, and the Holy Spirit makes alive to us the precious written word of God, the Bible,

thus enabling the transforming of our minds to be in conformity with the mind of Christ. We may sometimes
struggle and limp along the way of holiness, but as we
allow the word to be woven into our everyday life it starts
to be so much a part of us that it simply does not occur
to us to operate any other way. Walking in godliness becomes a matter of habit as, more and more, our lives become lost in Christ. Those of us who live in a contracting
church need, more than ever, to ensure that we are walking closely with Jesus, in the way of obedience to his
commands. This way of sanctification is not an interest-
ing philosophical idea. The business of being a mirror for
the attractively compelling light of Jesus entails a pattern
of living, a whole different approach to life from so much
that the world regards as 'normal'. The healing gospel
expresses the loving character of God, but it is also
tough, practical and very demanding, setting high stand-
ards. God offers us forgiveness for failure but he expects
us to stand up again and walk boldly onwards. Such a
pilgrimage is no sunny stroll through flowering countryside, yet its rewards are so deep and vast that every
struggling step is well worth it. To set out on that journey
is to find oneself wrestling with the darkness inside, fight-
ing the odd passing demon, taking the pilgrim way
through lands with bramble patches that trip and cut,
and stretches of deep, dry desert. But oh, the glimpses
of glory, and the company of pilgrims....

All this means that we have to start believing in the
God of miracles. Most of us, for most of the time, do not
have much expectancy about what God can do and is
willing to do. We may have a measure of hope —but
expectancy...? In the Old Testament we learn that a key

difference between all the false deities and the one, true God of Abraham, Isaac and Jacob is that he speaks and acts —unlike the dumb idols of the pagans.

Elijah lived during one of the many periods when God's people had been unfaithful and gone after other gods; in that respect it was a time like our own. He confronted the king, Ahab, with the accusation that he has abandoned the Lord's commands and has followed the baals. He told the king to summon the people from all over Israel to meet him on Mount Carmel, bringing the four hundred and fifty prophets of Baal and the four hundred prophets of Asherah who ate at Jezebel's table. These would be the prime bearers of unbelief. When they were all assembled, Elijah stood up before the people and said, "How long will you waver between two opinions? If the LORD is God, follow him; but if Baal is God, follow him."

There was no answer. Elijah then told the prophets of Baal to choose one of the bulls he had brought and prepare it for sacrificial burning. They were to call on the name of their god to send down fire from heaven, and Elijah would call on the name of the Lord. All agreed that the god who answered by fire would be the true God. The unbelieving prophets called on the name of Baal from morning until noon but nothing happened.

At midday Elijah began to taunt them. "Shout louder!" he said. "Surely he is a god! Perhaps he is deep in thought, or busy, or traveling. Maybe he is sleeping and must be awakened." This moment passed and they continued their frantic prophesying and rites of self-mutilation until the time for the evening sacrifice. There was no response, no one answered, no one paid attention to their desperate cries. Elijah then gathered the people around him and prayed for the fire to come and burn up his bull sacrifice. He had even soaked the pyre and the sacrifice with water to prove his point. The fire fell from heaven and all was consumed. This event took place at a crucial turning point in the religious life of Israel, but is recorded here to show one aspect: in the taunting of the opposition and in the watering of his own sacrifice, Elijah deliberately set out to attack the doubt of the unbelievers. The result was staggering. The people's doubt and unbelief was forcibly squashed by Elijah, and the fire came from God. To reflect on this marvellous example of expectancy in action is to learn something of how God wants his people to exercise faith.

Elijah did not climb Mount Carmel to pray for the people. He did not just offer to put king Ahab on his prayer list. He did not invite eight hundred and fifty false prophets to go up with him simply to preach to them. He took them to see the power of the living God. And what was the response of the watching crowds? It was just what so many of us are longing to hear in our streets and on the margins of the church: "The LORD—he is God! The LORD—he is God!"

Does the fire still come down? Does the Lord still show his mighty power? He is certainly doing so in the area of healing. Increasingly, we see his supernatural healing power at work. We are recovering an awareness that the preaching of the gospel is to be accompanied by the healing of the sick, as in New Testament times. For many years, the unchurched have been spoken of as white wheat fields ready for harvesting, people ready to be brought into the kingdom of God. But we need to return to the New Testament model for evangelism.

Jesus went through all the towns and villages, teaching in their synagogues, preaching the good news of the kingdom and healing every disease and sickness. When he saw the crowds, he had compassion on them, because they were harassed and helpless, like sheep without a shepherd. Then he said to his disciples, "The harvest is plentiful but the workers are few. Ask the Lord of the harvest, therefore, to send out workers into his harvest field."

He called his twelve disciples to him and gave them authority to drive out evil spirits and to heal every disease and sickness.

Matthew 9:35–10:1

Jesus taught, preached the kingdom and healed the sick. Healing and preaching were intimately linked. That was all part of the 'harvest' then, and it still is today. We are to be 'harvesters in healing'. Believers have a clear mandate from the Lord to heal the sick. Jesus' instructions to the twelve were: "As you go, preach this message: The kingdom of heaven is near. Heal the sick, raise the dead, cleanse those who have leprosy, drive out demons." (Matthew 10:7) The command to the disciples to heal the sick was never revoked, but was reiterated and reinforced.

He said to them, "Go into all the world and preach the good news to all creation. Whoever believes and is baptized will be saved, but whoever does not believe will be condemned. And these signs will accompany those who believe: In my name they will drive out demons; they will speak in new tongues; they will pick up snakes with their hands; and when they drink deadly poison, it will not hurt them at all; they will place their hands on sick people, and they will get well."

Mark 16:15–18

The command is clearly there in the word of God. He has revealed his will in the matter. Healing is to accompany the preaching of the word. How can we obey that command with true **expectancy** —really believing that he will act in power? Simply by accepting that it is Jesus who has given us authority and he who sends us, for he said:

"Peace be with you! As the Father has sent me, I am sending you.

John 20:21

The early church believed that God acts in power, and the church held this truth dear for its first one thousand years; but, since then.... We need to find a way to become truly expectant again and then we will see miracles in the home and the street; and on the margins of our congregations as much as on the mission field. We only need expectancy the size of a mustard seed and things start to happen, grace brings about amazing things. By his grace, when we begin to move in expectancy, heaven explodes. Why? —because the preached word was, and still is, to be accompanied by miracles.

I (Paul) will not venture to speak of anything except what Christ has accomplished through me in leading the Gentiles to obey God by what I have said and done— by the power of signs and miracles, through the power of the Spirit. So from Jerusalem all the way around to Illyricum, I have fully proclaimed the gospel of Christ.

Romans 15:18

4

Mustard Seeds and Expectations

The Bible is full of accounts of God's dealings with the saints of old, but dealing with sickness within one's own church family often seems like quite another matter. When faced with illness amongst friends and family today, it may not occur to us to stand on the promises of Scripture, and the reality of God's healing grace is too often far from our minds. We might have great 'God-confidence' when we read the Scriptures, but it sometime drains away when we are brought face to face with suffering. So where do we begin to look for encouragement?

With the possible exceptions of Isaiah and Moses, Elijah stands out as being Israel's most memorable prophet. We would probably remember him best for the shaming of hundreds of false prophets at the fiery sacrifice on the summit of Mount Carmel, and for his ascending by chariot into heaven in a whirlwind. But both he and his student Elisha had vibrant healing ministries, too! They seem to have known the key to unlocking something which we all crave: effective prayer. When they needed a miracle, it happened for them. The ninth century BC was a period of substantial turmoil in the life of the kingdom of Israel. Omri, the previous king, had set out to mix the true Israelite religion with Canaanite beliefs. King Ahab then carried on with the implementation of his father's multi-faith policy, establishing baal worship in his capital city of Samaria. Baal was held in awe in Canaan as the god of fertility and lord of the vine, and baalism taught that sexual immorality and the heavy consumption of alcohol were religious imperatives, promising richer harvests.

God raised up Elijah's ministry to deal with this crisis in Israel's spiritual life. How were these famous events in Elijah's ministry examples of effective praying? There seems to be a certain set of principles which have been recorded in Scripture by the Holy Spirit to help us to pray more effectively. Firstly, Elijah was totally committed. A talented and courageous man, he might have expected to have a promising career if he had converted to baalism, like so many others. But he did not. There was never a single moment when he considered converting to pagan faith —he would rather have died. Even his name reflects this strong attribute, meaning as it does, 'The Lord is my God'. He was locked up in his relationship with God. He remained absolutely committed in this way through thick and thin. He was a loyal servant to the true God of Israel. Neither was he afraid to steadfastly proclaim his commitment in public, along with the prophetic messages that God gave him for Ahab.

Secondly, Elijah was a man who communicated with

God; there was conversation between them. He had good 'inter-personal skills', the kind that enrich and deepen any vital relationship. In both prayer and spiritual commitment, this is an important quality. Whoever speaks *of* God, but never, or not very often, *to* God, easily leases their body and soul to idols. Elijah is depicted praying to God almost as regularly as he is reported preaching for God. He was a man of prayer. God continues to use people of prayer powerfully while they stay close through Jesus Christ to our Father in heaven.

Thirdly, Elijah was obedient. He was sent to a remote site to the east of the Jordan River, in the middle of a widespread famine. It was outside the borders of Israel that Elijah's hunger and thirst were satisfied. Miraculously, ravens came along to meet him twice a day, carrying enough bread and meat to satisfy his hunger, and a stream alongside his chosen resting place ran with good, fresh water. Eventually, this water supply dried up and God sent Elijah onwards to an even stranger place. It was the village of Zarephath, in Phoenicia, homeland of Ahab's wife, Jezebel, and the very centre of baal worship. That was not a congenial place to be, yet Elijah marched alone straight into the heart of enemy territory. Although God had withdrawn his blessings from Israel because of their devotion to baal worship, blessings are bestowed on a household in baal's own territory because a poor widow believed the word of God, ministered by the steadfast prophet. She expected the miraculous. His obedience was rewarded with a response from God which transformed that woman's spiritual and family life and restored her dead son to her alive.

Fourthly, Elijah was quite secure in the knowledge that

God would always be there for him. He had 'God-confidence'. We know nothing of Elijah's life before the events recorded in the Bible, other than his home town. The assumption is that the biblical stories about him probably occurred during his mature adulthood. However, because of his enormous God-confidence displayed on Mount Carmel, it is suspected that Elijah, an ordinary human being with our usual doubts and fears, would have proved to himself that God was trustworthy and reliable many times before, over and over again, possibly in events and circumstances not recorded in Scripture. His faith had to have been tried and tested and his confidence in God allowed to grow. He would have known experientially that the living God heard and answered his prayers. Lacking this quality of God-confidence is common. God said to Joshua:

> "Have I not commanded you? Be strong and courageous. Do not be terrified; do not be discouraged, for the LORD your God will be with you wherever you go."
>
> *Joshua 1:9*

Samuel Johnson wrote, 'Confidence is the first requisite to great undertakings.' Although this holds true for both the Christian and non-Christian alike, the Christian craves even more for this slightly different thing we are calling 'God-confidence'. Elijah on Mount Carmel seemed to be full of it. Moses lacked God-confidence when God called to him from the burning bush. If Joshua had plenty of God-confidence, God would not have needed to tell him not to be discouraged. Gideon is another person who most certainly lacked assurance; and God had to tell David not to fear over and over again. Until Jesus' disciples were filled with the Holy Spirit at Pentecost they had little if any confidence at all: when Jesus was taken captive, they ran away. St Paul gives us the impression that he must have had an abundance of God-confidence in every situation, yet God still had to send an angel to him when he was in prison to tell him not to fear. Being a little short on God-confidence is par for the course for most of us. How can we then go on budding and growing in this God-confidence? —by choosing to trust him, no matter how we are feeling, when faced with any situation that confronts us, however awful it is, we just keep saying to God, 'I choose to trust you in this situation, however appalling it might look.'

Fifthly, Elijah was quite specific in prayer When he discovered that the widow's son had stopped breathing, his heart broke for her and he interceded in prayer with an absolutely specific request for the life to be restored. God responded with a great miracle. There is always a place for general and contemplative prayer, and for elaborate prayers of adoration and thanksgiving, but these should never be at the expense of detailed prayers of confession and petition. If a man 'just like us' exercised a ministry of such powerful and effective prayer, then it must be possible for all of us.

An authentic faith, commitment to God, experience of God acting in our individual lives and a deep love for truth and compassion for those who suffer —these are the channels that God will flush through with his rivers of miraculous healing. We, the church, have not always made it easy for him to do so, but things are changing. In this century and the last, most of the world's denominations have begun slowly to restore the ministry of healing to its rightful place in the church's life. In the Church of England, for example, an Archbishops' Commission issued, in 1958, a report entitled *The Church's Healing Ministry,* and later Bishop Morris Maddocks founded the Acorn Christian Foundation. Further interest was reflected in *A Time to Heal,* a report commissioned by the House of Bishops in July 2000, the first such commission on healing in forty years.

The early years of the church in Britain and Ireland can offer us some useful insights into the restoration of this gentle ministry of grace. The level of expectation for healing in the church had fallen to almost nothing by the time Christianity became the official religion of the Roman Empire. This was so in Wales, even after Illtyd and Dubricius had seen a new depth and width of holiness at the Llantwit monastery. It is said that when one of the monks there was dying from the effects of a snake bite, his brothers gathered around him in his cell to practise the ministry to the dying. However, a deeply attentive Bible student called Samson seems to have assumed with staggering simplicity that, since Jesus and his followers healed sick people, then so should he. As a result of that rather simple and unintellectual conclusion he asked Illtyd if he could lay his hands on his dying brother and pray for his restoration to fullness of life. It seems that at first the holy Illtyd was a little suspicious that Samson's motive was to rival the pagan charms and spells of the druids, but he acquiesced. The brother was restored to health. The healing ministry began to revive in the Welsh Church, but this happened only very slowly.

Today, Christians rely on science to the almost total exclusion of God's supernatural power. The fact that science has its limitations in no way reduces people's complete faith and trust in it to keep them healthy. Medical science must be one of the greatest gifts of God to our modern generation, but our doctors are swamped with over-expectant patients and the church is in constant danger of losing sight of the power of the cross. To ignore our heartfelt longing to see things change for the better is to deny something at the base of our humanity.

As we see so much sickness, disability and suffering in others, our hearts are moved by compassion, and the simple question that must lie across the heart of every believer, of everyone who truly loves God and his people, is this: how can something be done? Can God use my prayers to heal the sick? Recognizing our own helplessness in the face of the distress of others, we begin to pray. It becomes almost a habit for mature Christians to find themselves in prayer, not always filled with expectancy that God will intervene in power, but with at least a measure of hope, whenever suffering comes to their attention. But understanding and experience often seem to conflict. As we pile our own philosophical theories on top of the Scriptures, we lose sight of the amazing breadth of grace, and the astonishing truth that God is willing to act in specific ways as we pray. So, with our lack of 'God-confidence', we lose any connection with the miraculous and begin to think that healing may not be possible. Our understanding of healing miracles follows our experience. If we do not see much, we do not expect much, and then we see even less. The early years of involvement in healing ministry are often given to the healing of the emotions, not much time being given to the physical, unless deep and blocking root causes are being sought. Over that time, if we are active in this ministry, a praying Christian might see, perhaps, one or two demonstrable healing miracles a year. If then you are fired by a fresh vision and intent to see God's glory fall in ways that would display Christ to the world, we could begin to ask the question, "What might happen to our view of things if we ignore all the perceived wisdom and charismatic rhetoric, and concentrate purely on the Scripture for inspiration?" What would happen if we forgot to be intellectual and street-wise, set aside all we may have seen in abuse of this gift and came to the Father heart of God in the wide-eyed and expectant innocence of childhood? How are we supposed to do the works that Jesus did?

> Then they asked him, "What must we do to do the works God requires?"
> Jesus answered, "The work of God is this: to believe in the one he has sent."
>
> *John 6:28*

To believe in the one he has sent? To take that saying at face value is simply to accept that Jesus Christ is indeed the Son of God and was sent by the Father. All Christians have held that belief, but in itself it does not fire the dynamite of heaven as Jesus is suggesting that it should. If it did, then we would surely be experiencing

God's gifts of healing with consummate ease and in very noticeable numbers. There is much more in that simple statement. Jesus was not just someone separate from the Father who succeeded in being obedient during his earthly ministry. The true Father of Jesus was not Joseph but Father God; through the action of God the Holy Spirit in the virgin's womb, God became flesh. So it is that we read the Gospels, watch Jesus, and stare straight into the heart of the Father. As Jesus' ministry progressed he healed everyone who asked him of every disease and sickness —all of them. So we know that it is the heart of the Father that all should receive healing. Of course the kingdom is here already, but not yet come in its fullness —there is more to come when Jesus returns as Lord of Lords and King of Kings, but in the meantime he has left the Holy Spirit to empower believers to continue this work and do even greater things than he did (i.e. more healings and other miracles, and in more places, than during Jesus' ministry on earth). To see the character and work of Jesus as revealing the Father's heart changes the way we view the sick and the way we pray. We begin to see those who suffer surrounded by a new sort of 'atmospheric pressure' —which is the will of God to heal.

In John 14:6 –11 we read,

Jesus answered, "I am the way and the truth and the life. No one comes to the Father except through me. If you really knew me, you would know my Father as well. From now on, you do know him and have seen him." Philip said, "Lord, show us the Father and that will be enough for us."

Jesus answered: "Don't you know me, Philip, even

after I have been among you such a long time? Anyone who has seen me has seen the Father. How can you say, 'Show us the Father'? Don't you believe that I am in the Father, and that the Father is in me? The words I say to you are not just my own. Rather, it is the Father, living in me, who is doing his work. Believe me when I say that I am in the Father and the Father is in me; or at least believe on the evidence of the miracles themselves."

There is only one set of conclusions that can be drawn from these sayings: that Jesus is the Son of God, and that he has been sent by the Father in heaven to do his works. What might they be? The works of God are miracles for change, for reclamation. The majority Christian reaction to the sufferings of others is to run and try to 'fetch' God in prayer. We turn to him, knocking on the door in some vague hope that he might be in 'the mood' today and that some change for the better may occur in the circumstances.

The starting point for us needs to be the incarnation. God expressed his Father heart of love for each and every human being when he sent his only-begotten Son in one particular historical moment. His Father heart is love and compassion itself. We know what that is like because Jesus has revealed it, and he told us so, when he said, 'He who has seen me has seen the Father.'

Jesus never did anything his heavenly Father did not do, or say or think. The only Son of the Father, he was in perfect unity with the Father's will. It follows then, and we must affirm and believe this in the utmost simplicity: that our heavenly Father's heart is still the same: his will, power and desire to heal the sick which was manifest in the life of Jesus is unchanged. Healing grace is not something we must go to heaven to fetch back for those who suffer. Healing is not something that experts in prayer know how to 'do' better than the rest of us. No, grace is rather like the atmospheric pressure that presses down on us at all angles, all of the time. Our heavenly Father's will to heal is constant and utterly reliable, and we know this because that is the truth we see revealed in Jesus, the Son of the Father.

When we do not see healing, the reason is not in the heart of God, but so often lies in our understanding: we are looking the wrong way. We are in a downward spiral of unbelief in the things of healing. Our understanding is being governed by our experience and our expectancy declines. If we pray with only a little hope and expect little, then we must not be surprised if we see little happen. Too readily we draw the conclusion that we cannot expect much, and our negative attitude is reinforced. At this point, either our hope declines even further or our prayers move away from hope towards desperation!

However, it is not hope or desperation that triggers heaven's response, but expectancy, firmly based on faith in the covenant promises in the word of God, and real confidence in the revealed truth about God's nature that we see in Jesus: that the heart of the Son shows us the heart of the Father. So the church's key in healing is not to learn how better to pray to organise the ministry, but how to open the door of the sufferer to allow the already present grace to flow in. Expectancy, persistence and humility are three vital keys to moving into all the healing work that God has in store for us.

5

The Heart of the Matter

Whatever our spirituality and church experience may have been, we will never get to grips with the real flavour of the healing grace of God unless we see the miracles of Jesus and the benefits of the cross as a focused reflection of God's heart for his hurting children.

Unhappily, our ability to allow this healing and restoring grace of Christ to flow through our ministry can be governed by the workings of our intellect. Instead of holding high the healing promises of God, as revealed in the life and death of Jesus, with child-like expectancy, we rationalize any apparent lack of God's works to fit our own lack of experience of these things. Because we do not see everyone being healed in the moment of our prayer, we may simply assume that God does not want to heal everybody. When approached by a hurting suppliant, too many of us retreat into our own healing philosophies with such statements as 'God's timing is perfect', or, 'Perhaps we should go for counselling and look for root causes.' The re-discovered truth is that our heavenly Father longs to heal all.

> At that time Jesus said, "I praise you, Father, Lord of heaven and earth, because you have hidden these things from the wise and learned, and revealed them to little children. Yes, Father, for this was your good pleasure."
>
> *Matthew 11:25–26*

> At that time the disciples came to Jesus and asked, "Who is the greatest in the kingdom of heaven?"
>
> He called a little child and had him stand among them. And he said: "I tell you the truth, unless you change and become like little children, you will never enter the kingdom of heaven."
>
> *Matthew 18:1–3*

That is the requirement —one of the simplest and yet most difficult things. To see his power released, we have to think again about our understanding of the Christian healing ministry, and begin to approach our Father like a six-year old expecting presents, with an uncluttered and child-like trust.

As we come to grips with this, we recall first that the Israelites always understood that the Messiah would be a healer.

> Say to those with fearful hearts, "Be strong, do not fear; your God will come, he will come with vengeance; with divine retribution he will come to save

you." Then will the eyes of the blind be opened and
the ears of the deaf unstopped. Then will the lame
leap like a deer, and the mute tongue shout for
joy. Water will gush forth in the wilderness and
streams in the desert.

Isaiah 35:4–6

If Jesus is truly God incarnate, God made man, who has
revealed the Father, then our God must surely be a
healer. The name of Jesus was chosen by God, Scripture
records, because he had come to save his people. The
notion that the Messiah might save only part of the
human being, his soul, and that only at death, would have
been foreign to the Israelite mind. The Messiah was to be
someone who would bring salvation of body, mind and
spirit. Jesus, the Messiah, always granted immediate
healing to everyone who asked him for it. He healed
because it is God's nature to heal; it is Jesus' work to
heal. Indeed, when John asked from prison for
confirmation of Jesus' Messiahship, Jesus replied by
emphasising the works of God:

After Jesus had finished instructing his twelve
disciples, he went on from there to teach and preach
in the towns of Galilee.

When John heard in prison what Christ was doing,
he sent his disciples to ask him, "Are you the one
who was to come, or should we expect someone
else?"

Jesus replied, "Go back and report to John what
you hear and see: The blind receive sight, the lame
walk, those who have leprosy are cured, the deaf

hear, the dead are raised, and the good news is
preached to the poor."

Matthew 11:1–5

When religious leaders repeatedly demanded from
Jesus some proof of his Messiahship, he told them about
the miracles:

The Jews gathered around him, saying, "How long
will you keep us in suspense? If you are the Christ,
tell us plainly."
   Jesus answered, "I did tell you, but you do not
believe. The miracles I do in my Father's name
speak for me...."

John 10:24–25

And in John 10:37,38:

"Do not believe me unless I do what my Father
does. But if I do it, even though you do not believe
me, believe the miracles, that you may know and
understand that the Father is in me, and I in the
Father."

Obviously, the willingness, power and ability to heal all
the sick among us is part of the nature of Jesus Christ
and, therefore, of our Father God today. In Jesus'
ministry on earth, people came to hear what he had to
say, and to be healed of all their illnesses. No great
instructions were given about 'God's timing', nor is it
suggested that, somehow, sickness is redemptive. There
are few occasions where 'hidden roots' have to be

cleansed out before healing takes place, and even in those few instances it comes quickly. Nor were there any grandiose statements that death is the most wonderful healing of all, and there is no suggestion by Jesus that anyone is not good enough to receive healing. He simply heals!

Then he said to the man, "Stretch out your hand." So he stretched it out and it was completely restored, just as sound as the other. But the Pharisees went out and plotted how they might kill Jesus. Aware of this, Jesus withdrew from that place. Many followed him, and he healed all their sick....

Matthew 12:13–15

As soon as they got out of the boat, people recognized Jesus. They ran throughout that whole region and carried the sick on mats to wherever they heard he was. And wherever he went—into villages, towns or countryside—they placed the sick in the marketplaces. They begged him to let them touch even the edge of his cloak, and all who touched him were healed.

Mark 6:54–56

During a three year ministry of teaching and freely offering the restoring gifts of God, it is clear that Jesus did what the Father willed to be done —perfectly. We must conclude that God is still longing to see the work of healing done.

Jesus gave them this answer: "I tell you the truth, the Son can do nothing by himself; he can do only what he sees his Father doing, because whatever the Father does the Son also does. For the Father loves the Son and shows him all he does. Yes, to your amazement he will show him even greater things than these."

John 5:19–20

At the end of his time on earth, Jesus came to Calvary. Everything flows from how we learn the patience to stand under the cross of Jesus, because when we are there we see what he sees: the infinite glory and love of the Father. Calvary is where the healing fountains start, and any understanding of healing grace begins with our understanding of the death of Jesus Christ.

The truth of the crucifixion has always been the heart of the matter —all through the centuries, and today. It is on the cross that Jesus became the 'last Adam', the last man in the line for our evil inheritance, the last man of a whole world-wide civilisation. Then the scene changed. When he was raised from the dead, Jesus became the second man, the new Adam, the head of an entirely new race, a species of 'resurrection people'. The clear dividing line between the old and the new order is the cross. Now, when a person receives the crucified, risen Jesus as Lord and Saviour and is born again by the Spirit of God, a new creation has taken place. Old things pass away and there is new life for the believer. The crucified, risen Lord Jesus Christ is himself the gateway to the kingdom. When he has given us that new birth, we are eligible for all the benefits of his new covenant.

Pass through, pass through the gates! Prepare the way for the people. Build up, build up the highway! Remove the stones. Raise a banner for the nations. The LORD has made proclamation to the ends of the earth: "Say to the Daughter of Zion, 'See, your Saviour comes! See, his reward is with him, and his recompense accompanies him.'"

They will be called the Holy People, the Redeemed of the LORD; and you will be called Sought After, the City No Longer Deserted.

Isaiah 62:10–12

What exactly is the nature of the actual work accomplished by Christ on the cross, this revelation of the godhead? Isaiah 53 is the great prophetic picture of the atonement, given seven hundred years before Jesus' glorious death. In verse 6 we read,

We all, like sheep, have gone astray, each of us has turned to his own way; and the LORD has laid on him the iniquity of us all.

We have all turned to our own ways, and our methods of doing things, which are not God's ways. More than this, natural, unregenerate man is born with the stain of Adam's sin, an orientation which has self rather than God at the heart of the human spirit. Until we are born again, our great need is for a Saviour and Deliverer who will put his Spirit within us. In coming to this earth as a man, God himself makes that provision for all who turn to Jesus in repentance and faith, trusting in him alone. So it is that

Jesus on the cross at Calvary is the focal point for the meeting of all the iniquity of the entire Adamic race. The work of Christ in this stunning place is to redeem us from the curse of the law by becoming a curse for us.

> Christ redeemed us from the curse of the law by becoming a curse for us, for it is written: 'Cursed is everyone who is hung on a tree.' He redeemed us in order that the blessing given to Abraham might come to the Gentiles through Christ Jesus, so that by faith we might receive the promise of the Spirit.
>
> *Galatians 3:13–14*

What curse? What blessing? What is this great exchange that tears through the veil between heaven and earth in the moment of Jesus' dying? Slung in the utmost vulnerability between thieves, and exposed to the mockery of the world, an exchange between two things takes place before our gaze: cursing and blessing. Here is the curse of human disobedience and all its evil effects, which was placed upon Jesus.

> "However, if you do not obey the LORD your God and do not carefully follow all his commands and decrees I am giving you today, all these curses will come upon you and overtake you: You will be cursed in the city and cursed in the country. Your basket and your kneading trough will be cursed. The fruit of your womb will be cursed, and the crops of your land, and the calves of your herds and the lambs of your flocks...."
>
> *Deuteronomy 28:15ff.*

As Jesus hung on the cross, he actually became that curse and it died with him. He completely destroyed the curse so that we might become the blessing. Jesus, the eternal Son of God, on the cross, took upon himself all the evil that was due by justice to the entire human race: to Adam and all his descendants including ourselves, so that, in return, the one who believes in Jesus Christ may receive all the blessings of God's kingdom, rather than eternal death. This is the great exchange.

> Surely he took up our infirmities and carried our sorrows, yet we considered him stricken by God, smitten by him, and afflicted. But he was pierced for our transgressions, he was crushed for our iniquities; the punishment that brought us peace was upon him, and by his wounds we are healed.
>
> *Isaiah 53:4–5*

We may divide the great exchange into five sub-sections, thus making it a little easier for us to grasp its amazing extent. Firstly, our punishment was exchanged for God's peace. As he died, Jesus bore the punishment that was due to us for our transgressions and all our iniquities, our acts of rebellion. All the punishment for every contrary act committed by every member of the entire Adamic race was brought onto Jesus. Not one sinful act was left out. The blessing now available, the alternative to eternal punishment, is summed up in the word 'peace'. In place of punishment, there is peace for the believer, reconciliation and pardon; and God's justice was satisfied at Calvary.

But now in Christ Jesus you who once were far away have been brought near through the blood of Christ. For he himself is our peace, who has made the two one and has destroyed the barrier, the dividing wall of hostility....

Ephesians 2:13,14

Secondly, our poverty has been exchanged for God's riches: that poverty with which we were cursed in our disobedience.

Because you did not serve the LORD your God joyfully and gladly in the time of prosperity, therefore in hunger and thirst, in nakedness and dire poverty, you will serve the enemies the LORD sends against you. He will put an iron yoke on your neck until he has destroyed you.

Deuteronomy 28:47,48

The curse of poverty, broken down for us into component parts—hunger, thirst and nakedness—adds up to a state of total and absolute destitution, and that curse came onto Jesus, too.

For you know the grace of our Lord Jesus Christ, that though he was rich, yet for your sakes he became poor, so that you through his poverty might become rich.

II Corinthians 8:9

Jesus took our poverty onto the cross so that we might

have his riches. He was hungry, not having eaten for almost twenty-four hours. He himself said, "I thirst." He was naked, for the soldiers had taken all his clothes for themselves, casting lots for his seamless robe. He was totally bereft of everything, a picture of total poverty, exhausting the curse. Jesus, who was rich with heaven's riches, became poor on the cross so that we might in turn share in his riches. This is the grace of God.

> And God is able to make all grace abound to you, so that in all things at all times, having all that you need, you will abound in every good work.
>
> *II Corinthians 9:8*

This is amazing abundance. This is the level of God's provision through Jesus Christ, as a direct result of the cross. God is able to make all grace abound towards us and it comes only through Jesus Christ, through the cross.

> For the law was given through Moses; grace and truth came through Jesus Christ.
>
> *John 1:17*

Thirdly, Jesus has exchanged our mortality for a share in his immortality.

> But we see Jesus, who was made a little lower than the angels, now crowned with glory and honour, because he suffered death, so that by the grace of God he might taste death for everyone.
>
> *Hebrews 2:9*

Jesus, our substitute, has tasted every man's death on Calvary, the punishment due to us, because the wages of sin is death. He has paid our wages by his atoning death, because, 'God made him who had no sin to be sin for us, so that in him we might become the righteousness of God' (II Corinthians 5:21). Jesus has died as our representative, on our behalf. He has tasted death so that you and I might have eternal life.

> For God so loved the world that he gave his one and only Son, that whoever believes in him shall not perish but have eternal life.
>
> *John 3:16*

Jesus has paid the final penalty for our breaking the law, which is death. He has tasted death for each one of us. He drank the bitter cup to its dregs, the cup of which he said, "Abba, Father... everything is possible for you. Take this cup from me. Yet not what I will, but what you will" (Mark 14:36).

In fulfilling the Father's will, Jesus drained the bitter cup of death to the last drop. He exhausted death and by doing so has victory over it, and has made immortality available to the believer.

Fourthly, through Jesus we have been offered his righteousness in exchange for our own efforts to be holy.

> For we know that our old self was crucified with him so that the body of sin might be done away with, that we should no longer be slaves to sin....
>
> *Romans 6:6*

> But seek first first his kingdom and his righteousness, and all these things will be given to you as well.
>
> *Matthew 6:33*

The difficulty for us has always lain in the fact that the only righteousness acceptable in heaven is the righteousness of God; this is received through faith in Jesus Christ.

> All of us have become like one who is unclean, and all our righteous acts are like filthy rags; we all shrivel up like a leaf, and like the wind our sins sweep us away.
>
> *Isaiah 64:6*

Without faith in Jesus Christ, all we might ever be able to do would be as filthy rags, whereas what all people need is God's righteousness —which we have in his sight when we receive new birth, made possible by grace through faith, as a result of the cross. God requires that we do not depend on those filthy rags of our own religious activities and good works, but that we acknowledge we are sinful, believe Jesus paid the price for our sin on the cross, and receive him as saviour and Lord —and so become clothed with his righteousness. Our old, naturally rebellious, naturally self-orientated human nature was crucified with Jesus. He, himself, experienced that old human separation from the Father. He underwent that for us so that we should not have to live in that terrible state for all eternity. The way out from under a life of sin is to know for yourself, personally, that on the cross that sinful nature was killed.

There are so many ways in which human beings try to work out a salvation for themselves. Some of them are religious; some are based on a misguided belief in human philosophies, or confidence in people, but we cannot change the nature of the rebellious heart of mankind. No programme of human reform will ever achieve that. God's provision for dealing with sin is simple: execution. In truth, that remedy has already taken place. As Jesus died, our old, rebellious nature died in him.

Here is the miraculous exchange: that as we receive Jesus by faith as our only Lord and Saviour, the old nature dies, a new nature, a Christ-like nature, a more transparent life is given to the new believer. The nature of Christ then indwells the believer's heart.

> Therefore, since we have been justified through faith, we have peace with God through our Lord Jesus Christ, through whom we have gained access by faith into this grace in which we now stand.
>
> *Romans 5:1–2a*

Fifthly, our sicknesses and pains have been taken on the cross so that we might receive healing through Jesus' wounds. He suffered terrible flogging and the imposition of the crown of thorns, and was crucified. As those terrible wounds were inflicted, so the covenant remedy for the pains and sicknesses of the whole human race was given. In accepting those things, he has made provision for our complete healing.

On the cross was a bleeding, torn, wounded body, bereft of all things, who took upon himself the punishment due for all our sins, as well as our curses and our poverty —all this so that we might be forgiven and reconciled with the Father, as well as inheriting his peace, receiving healing, deliverance from evil, and abundant life. So Jesus said: "It is finished."

Is there a way for everyone into God's provisions through this great exchange?

But what does it say? "The word is near you; it is in your mouth and in your heart," that is, the word of faith we are proclaiming: That if you confess with your mouth, "Jesus is Lord," and believe in your heart that God raised him from the dead, you will be saved. For it is with your heart that you believe and are justified, and it is with your mouth that you confess and are saved.

Romans 10:8–10

'Salvation' includes every benefit obtained for the believer by Jesus Christ on the cross. To enter into this salvation by faith we must speak it out with our mouth and then believe it in our heart. He bore our griefs and carried our sorrows and by his wounds we are healed — he was physically wounded so that we might be healed.

So the heavenly Father, our healer, sent his son, Jesus, to earth to show us his nature —and we saw the healing of the sick. Just as it is God's nature to love—something that he cannot stop doing—so it is his nature to heal. He came as suffering servant and saviour, yet everything was placed under his feet. Our thinking needs to come into line with this revealed truth, rather than our own speculations, theories and philosophies.

Jesus will return and be seen by all as Lord of lords and

King of kings. In the meantime, he has commissioned his people—the church; the company of believers—to preach the saving gospel and to heal the sick.

6

Foundations

One aspect of the Christian life will usually need some attention before we can be effective for God. There have been countless sermons, thousands of conference lectures and many books written on the subject of *unforgiveness*. Yet the world is full of the pain and anger that linger on, in the wake of real (and imagined) wrongs committed against people. The burden of unforgiveness is very great, and carried by many. But we know full well that, by nursing unforgiveness, we turn away from Jesus the healer, however much we may long to be healed. We may struggle to be a forgiving community, and sometimes we achieve it, much to the joy of our own hearts and our Father in heaven, but there are times when it seems almost impossible to forgive fully and finally. It is not that the sin against us was particularly huge —it might have been anything, from some hurt that threatened the wholeness of our personality to the point of devastation, or at the other end of the spectrum, it might have been a silly misunderstanding that rankled for years. From the one extreme to the other, large sins and little ones, there are those who find that completely forgiving them is extremely hard. We can walk out of a valley of tears where the land was barren and the dry bones had no life, and travel over the hill into greener pastures and new abundance of wholeness of heart. Then, for no apparent reason, we can find ourselves wandering, unwittingly, back into all the mess and pain again. What is the reason for this? Why can we not let go? What is holding us back from the freedom offered by the gospel? At one level, we encounter the buffeting of our relationships with other people, and fall into unforgiveness from time to time. We want to lash out in our anger, complain, ridicule and hurt until someone—or the Holy Spirit at work within—reminds us of the sin of unforgiveness; and then we begin to let go of the unforgiveness again, and repent. From time to time, we stray into that territory where justice is sought for and prevails, and it is the land where what is called 'the flesh' batters us. We may experience conversion, re-birth and baptism in the Holy Spirit. We may discover new and exciting worship styles, a new openness of affection with other Christians, and a whole new way to hear the Scriptures, but at a certain level there is something in us which is the old, rebellious self. The Bible calls all that is opposed to God's will 'the flesh', and the battle against it is a lifetime's struggle. This is well explained, and the way in which we can engage successfully in that warfare is set out with great clarity, in a book by Hartmut Kopsch, entitled *The Struggle* (Terra Nova).

Our minds, wills and emotions need to operate not just on the legal model, requiring justice, but in line with the

New Testament dispensation, where grace and forgiveness flow ever more powerfully; where the river of God, overflows with healing and restoration. So what stops us? Why can so many not make the inviting step up into the river that flows from the foot of the cross? Why do our feet feel held down on the floor? It is a nail in the foot that keeps us in bondage: a nail called a bitter root.

> See to it that no one misses the grace of God and that no bitter root grows up to cause trouble and defile many.
>
> *Hebrews 12:15.*

Does it make us miss the grace of God? Most assuredly it does: it keeps us from the river. Does it cause trouble and defile many? It most certainly lies at the heart of much evil gossip, spreading poison through the flock and defiling them, as they verbalise critical views of each other, which are often twisted. And what of us who have bitter roots and do not recognise them for what they are?

> You, therefore, have no excuse, you who pass judgment on someone else, for at whatever point you judge the other, you are condemning yourself, because you who pass judgment do the same things.
>
> *Romans 2:1*

As we pass judgment we are guilty of a sin, not only against those who have hurt us but against Christ, because we are spoiling his bride. We devour our own flesh. Here, then, is a major key to releasing forgiveness in one's mind and body, forcing the emotional and physical 'torturers' to leave us. We give up trying, for a moment, to forgive those who have inflicted pain on us; and turn to Christ, asking forgiveness from him for sinning against him by allowing a bitter root to grow up inside us. Then we can step forward and take our rightful place where the healing rivers flow —until next time! But then this is the glory of God's forgiving and unconditional love —we can return to his living water again and again.

The key to walking into this everyday arrival of healing miracles under God's grace and mercy towards his children can be found in Peter's address to the house of Cornelius.

> You know the message God sent to the people of Israel, telling the good news of peace through Jesus Christ, who is Lord of all. You know what has happened throughout Judea, beginning in Galilee after the baptism that John preached—how God anointed Jesus of Nazareth with the Holy Spirit and power, and how he went around doing good and healing all who were under the power of the devil, because God was with him.
>
> *Acts 10:36–38*

There are clear principles here, by which we are to walk and minister under the anointing of the Holy Spirit. Firstly, we must accept the baptism of the Holy Spirit for ourselves, not in any light fashion, but in the deep conviction that we all need to be transformed more and more into the likeness of Christ. That means we are to allow him to begin to change our character to be more

like his, but it also means that we must do his works —
continue his ministry on this earth.

Secondly, we must go about doing good. What comes
out of us has to be love, joy, patience, kindness and so on,
the fruit of the Holy Spirit working within. That will only
happen if we go on being filled with the Holy Spirit, and
are walking in obedience to Jesus, keeping close to him
and worshipping him. Faith sometimes means stepping
out and taking risks, and this is only too apparent in the
healing of the sick. To pray aloud, and specifically for
healing, in the supplicant's presence, holds a greater risk
of losing face than many of us are prepared for. But God
is waiting for us on the very edge of our expectancy; he
will uphold us and help us the instant we start to really
take a step of trust and do what he has told us in the New
Testament to do. In the healing context, we must remember that compassion is as essential as faith for the release
of the anointing.

> A man with leprosy came to him and begged him on
> his knees, "If you are willing, you can make me
> clean."
> Filled with compassion, Jesus reached out his
> hand and touched the man. "I am willing," he said.
> "Be clean!"
>
> *Mark 1:40–41*

When the man received the healing touch of Jesus, who
was full of compassion, the leprosy left him and he was
cured.

Thirdly, the healing minister must throw off his/her
knowledge and past experiences of praying with others

where that experience has not yielded fruit. Each assumed 'failure' reduces expectancy. We must live in the simplest child-like trust, knowing deeply, in our hearts, that God is willing to heal because he has revealed that to be his will; and that his heart is to heal all disease, not to withhold his hand, for any reason, but to bring restoration of the body and mind, and to put a new Spirit within us.

We need to accept confidently the delegated authority to heal the sick on God's behalf; to minister in his power, under his leading, and in an atmosphere of worship. He has given authority to mankind to rule over the things of the earth; and to his disciples he has given authority to heal the sick; and we need to develop the stomach for the activity of exercising that authority. If we do not (and this can mean a huge change of attitude as we begin to understand the power in the new creation at work in us) then we will be left only with despairing, forlorn prayers: a feeble, powerless shadow of what God has called us to do in the name of Jesus.

Most of us, when praying with others, do not use our God-given authority over sickness, and our ministry is much the poorer for that. There are moments when we call on the Lord to heal, but there are many times when we do well to address the illness itself, speaking to the condition, rebuking it; speaking, as Jesus did, to the person; speaking healing; commanding the sick body to come into order. We must consider how Jesus ministered, and how the disciples ministered, according to the Gospel accounts; and how the apostolic healing ministry was exercised, as described in Acts, taking those patterns as our models for healing ministry.

Often, we hear intercessory prayer when the direct exercising of authority is what is needed. "Lord, we would just ask you to touch this lady's ear and bring hearing back to it. She has been in our choir for ten years, and we thank you for her, etc., etc...." should instead be, "I tell you in Jesus' name to come into order," or some similarly direct word, addressed to the condition. Jesus said, "Be opened" (just a single word of command in the original language); and a brief word spoken directly with authority, under the anointing, is better than dozens of words about the condition, the person and their frailties or virtues. God is perfectly well aware of what is wrong with the sufferer. He is looking to you, his servant, whom he has empowered by his Spirit and instructed to do the works that Jesus did, to step out in faith and *exercise* that delegated authority in faith. Taking authority in Jesus' name, and speaking directly in this way is the greatest risk of all to the minister's image and self-esteem, if things do not seem to work out; but God is there, working on the very edge of our expectancy, and it is all a matter of leaning on him rather than on our own understanding. Jesus is enthroned in heaven, and if he is also enthroned in our hearts, as our king, our saviour and Lord, then our hearts are set on what he wants. From his throne in heaven pours the grace of God —and salvation, healing and deliverance flow, in Jesus' name.

At a practical level, in our ministry we have identified seven steps, which, whilst they are not in themselves keys to releasing the flow of the healing river of God, do serve to assist the minister in getting his or her own attitude to ministry right, and to avoid some basic pitfalls.

1. Bless the supplicant as appropriate —e.g. bless him or her to receive all that God has for them, to be at peace. Anointing with oil may be appropriate at this point, as it signifies that something is about to happen and serves to raise the level of corporate expectancy.

2. Interview, with such gentle questions as, "Where does it hurt?" "How long have you been like this?" "How did it happen?" "How much can you move it?"

3. Deal quickly with any unforgiveness and shock that may be lying there unseen, as a result of an accident; e.g. "Do you agree with me that....? There will be no need and no time for long lectures on the subject of forgiveness which display the minister's knowledge of the subject. When Jesus is present to heal, the work must be swiftly undertaken. Break off the curse of any shock as it may be covering over the trauma and keeping it secret.

4. Pray concisely, specifically, and with authority. The use of any medical knowledge about the condition may be helpful here, though do not get bogged down in detail.

5. The minister's persistence at this stage will be valued in heaven. Gentle enquiries, e.g. "Is that any different?" "Can you do something that you couldn't do before?"

6. 'Soaking' prayer may be helpful at this point, even if initial benefits are already manifesting. Continual prayer that welcomes the Holy Spirit into the situation will help to 'lock in' or seal the healing. If benefits are not yet seen, then 'soaking' prayer may often be the key to going on receiving healing. Keep enquiring until it is time to stop.

7. If nothing seems to have changed, always provide further encouragement, e.g. "You must keep on asking for prayer at every opportunity." Persistence has to be encouraged.

Will all this lead to instant and large scale results? Will the would-be minister's prayers become completely effective overnight? It would seem that, more often than not, the answer to that is no. God does not appear to require his 'first-year medical students' to do brain surgery for him; we walk into these things as our own expectancy, persistence and humility grow. We may follow Peter on the same journey into the miraculous. His first step was not a miracle, simply an act of obedience:

> One day as Jesus was standing by the Lake of Gennesaret, with the people crowding around him and listening to the word of God, he saw at the water's edge two boats, left there by the fishermen, who were washing their nets. He got into one of the boats, the one belonging to Simon, and asked him to put out a little from shore. Then he sat down and taught the people from the boat.
>
> *Luke 5:1ff.*

Simon was asked to do something well within his own proven ability: to push a boat out a little way and hold it there. This would have been an everyday task for a fisherman, but it did enable Jesus to preach in safety. This must, however, have been the highest example of the ministry of the Word —holding up a platform from which God himself might address the people. The next step followed soon afterwards:

> When he had finished speaking, he said to Simon, "Put out into deep water, and let down the nets for

a catch." Simon answered, "Master, we've worked hard all night and haven't caught anything. But because you say so, I will let down the nets." When they had done so, they caught such a large number of fish that their nets began to break.

Luke 5:4

What a miracle! —despite Simon's reluctance to go fishing with nets that he had just cleaned and mended — and after an entire night of wasted effort! Even faced with that reluctant obedience Jesus was able to work a miracle for all to see.

Peter's third step, into a new level of obedience, much later in Jesus' ministry, was out of his boat and onto the stormy waters of the lake.

Jesus immediately said to them: "Take courage! It is I. Don't be afraid."

"Lord, if it's you," Peter replied, "tell me to come to you on the water."

"Come," he said. Then Peter got down out of the boat, walked on the water and came toward Jesus.

Matthew 14:27–29

Here we notice that his talking to Jesus was not very miraculous, and neither are most of our prayers today. Climbing over the gunwale of the boat is not a miraculous feat for a fisherman. Even placing his foot towards the water, with every intention of trying to walk there, is not supernatural. The whole episode only becomes miraculous as Peter places his weight on his extended foot. It is at that point, when he begins to take a risk in response to

Jesus' summons, and to show a child-like expectancy of success, that God works the miracle.

Much later, long after that lesson about trusting and expecting has been learnt, the risen Lord Jesus has appeared repeatedly, and the Holy Spirit has come upon Peter, he could confidently minister healing to the sick. We recall those amazingly confident words, "Silver or gold I do not have, but what I have I give you. In the name of Jesus Christ of Nazareth, walk" (See Acts 3:3ff). Peter had first needed to learn to trust Jesus in practical ways, for his life, his safety, his whole being. We see that, as Peter ministered, he moved with quiet and powerful assurance; complete expectancy and trust — based on the believer's own mandate from the Lord to take authority over sickness, in Jesus' name. Peter is not succeeding here only because he has been told in the past by Jesus to do this sort of thing, but because of a deep, sure knowledge that this is the very work of God which he has been called to do, empowered by the flow of the Holy Spirit, released at Pentecost. Now we see that in Peter's walk into the miraculous life, healing the sick has become normal work for him to do.

> People brought the sick into the streets and laid them on beds and mats so that at least Peter's shadow might fall on some of them as he passed by. Crowds gathered also from the towns around Jerusalem, bringing their sick and those tormented by evil spirits, and all of them were healed.
>
> *Acts 5:15,16*

None of us can survive in this wonderful ministry by

clinging onto some sort of triumphalism: a humble and teachable spirit is of the essence. Worship, prayer and a hungry reaching of the soul, further and further into the things of Christ, make our hearts assured of the amazing Fatherhood of God, and fill us with a longing to see the gospel message proclaimed in its fullness.

7

The Keys of Release

Contrary to popular opinion in some quarters, ministers with well-known names are not the only anointed ones in matters of divine healing. Certain individuals may minister effectively for the healing of various illnesses, but such gifting is often due to their own levels of faith in these areas. There are also what Paul terms 'gifts of healing' (I Cor.12:9) and some are anointed for particular forms of ministry. Yet the whole church is called to heal the sick—every Christian, you and me included! What we need are the keys to release that latent power of the cross, and we shall discover that there is, most certainly, incomparably great power for us who believe. It is the same power that raised our Lord from the dead. We can see the pattern of growth of this inclusive ministry of healing, as it is set out in the New Testament.

First, there are the instructions given to the twelve:

He called them to him and gave them authority to drive out evil spirits and to heal every disease and sickness.... As you go, preach this message: 'The kingdom of heaven is near.' Heal the sick, raise the dead, cleanse those who have leprosy, drive out demons. Freely you have received, freely give.

Matthew 10:1

Then the seventy-two are commissioned and sent out:

After this the Lord appointed seventy-two others and sent them two by two ahead of him to every town and place where he was about to go. He told them, "The harvest is plentiful, but the workers are few. Ask the Lord of the harvest, therefore, to send out workers into his harvest field...."

Luke 10:1

and in verse 9 — 'Heal the sick who are there and tell them, "The kingdom of God is near you."'

Then, in Luke 10:17, the seventy-two returned with joy and said, "Lord, even the demons submit to us in your name."

In the Acts of the Apostles, the whole church was involved.

Those who had been scattered preached the word wherever they went. Philip went down to a city in Samaria and proclaimed the Christ there. When the crowds heard Philip and saw the miraculous signs he did, they all paid close attention to what he said. With shrieks, evil spirits came out of many, and

many paralytics and cripples were healed. So there
was great joy in that city.

Acts 8:4–8

To move into a position of real faith in God's power to
heal today, a place of daily abundance in healing
miracles, often entails a struggle. The walk in the Spirit
along this journey into the healing heart of the Father is
a walk towards the things of God and away from the
world, and that means it is a battle; there is stress and
struggle in it, because we battle against worldly, fleshly,
soulish thinking about the power of God. We fail to trust
his promises. Our minds are still tainted with intellectual
scepticism, our hearts often lack that expectancy which
is needed. We have to know and believe that, 'with God
all things are possible', and expect him to act in
accordance with his own self-revelation. Expectancy is
the little fish swimming upstream against the flowing
current of popular opinion. It is as though the other
angry, ugly faced, skeletal fish of scepticism swim
downstream, floating with the current, while the little
expectant fish swims doggedly onwards in the other
direction. If he relaxes for so much as a moment, he
begins to be swept downstream by the prevailing current,
even though he would still be facing in the right
direction. He must press forward.

As Jesus went on from there, two blind men followed
him, calling out, "Have mercy on us, Son of David!"
When he had gone indoors, the blind men came to
him, and he asked them, "Do you believe that I am
able to do this?"

"Yes, Lord," they replied.

Then he touched their eyes and said, "According to your faith will it be done to you."

Matthew 9:27–30

Never in all the records of Jesus' healing grace is the first of these keys so obviously expressed. He asks the two blind men if they believe in his ability to heal. As they confessed their belief [of which expectancy was a key ingredient] they were healed. The modern usage of the word 'faith' denotes a person's religion, and the depth by which he believes its truth claims. So to suggest, even by implication, that someone needs more faith can be perceived as unkind or hurtful. In some contexts it can simply pile on false guilt, though on other occasions it is certainly appropriate to encourage others to have faith. Jesus did so! We must be sensitive to the Holy Spirit's leading in these things.

The theme of expectancy occurs so often in the Gospels. Consider another example:

"Who touched me?" Jesus asked.

When they all denied it, Peter said, "Master, the people are crowding and pressing against you."

But Jesus said, "Someone touched me; I know that power has gone out from me." Then the woman, seeing that she could not go unnoticed, came trembling and fell at his feet. In the presence of all the people, she told why she had touched him and how she had been instantly healed. Then he said to her, "Daughter, your faith has healed you. Go in peace."

Luke 8:45–48

The implication is undeniable: the woman's faith (which included her *expectancy*) when she touched Jesus played a major role in her healing. At a deep level, she *knew* Jesus would make it happen.

To emphasize the point, Luke immediately goes on to relate another even more dramatic healing which, again, is marked by expectancy.

> While Jesus was still speaking, someone came from the house of Jairus, the synagogue ruler. "Your daughter is dead," he said. "Don't bother the teacher any more."
>
> Hearing this, Jesus said to Jairus, "Don't be afraid; just believe, and she will be healed."
>
> *Luke 8:49–50*

Jairus was clearly shown by Jesus' words that his believing [which clearly was to include expectancy that healing would take place as a result of Jesus' ministry] was significant in the raising of his daughter from the dead. "Just believe," Jesus tells him, "and she will be healed."

Jesus would hardly have enjoined believing if it did not matter!

> Jesus stepped into a boat, crossed over and came to his own town. Some men brought to him a paralytic, lying on a mat. When Jesus saw their faith, he said to the paralytic, "Take heart, son; your sins are forgiven."
>
> *Matthew 9:1*

Those who brought the paralytic to Jesus demonstrated a powerful *expectancy* that he would heal. Yet again, the need for expectant faith to be expressed and acted upon is dramatically confirmed.

Many Christians might say they believe that Jesus *can* heal the sick, or even that he does heal sometimes. But often this is far from being hope in the biblical sense. The Bible clearly shows it is his will to heal all who come to him —believing, trusting, confidently *expecting* that he will do as he has promised. When sickness strikes down some dear one, we bang loudly on the gates of heaven with desperate prayers for God to come down and sort out the awfulness of the situation. God is good, and his grace is amazing. He hears the cries of his people. But something more is needed in healing ministry. Those ministering, and as many as possible who are involved in the situation, need to really expect that Jesus will really act. Before we release such expectancy in the 'full assurance of faith' we may need to repent of our unbelief.

This is not a matter of performing some mental acrobatics to convince ourselves of something! It is certainly not 'mind over matter'. What we are talking about is a deeper believing in the authority and power of Jesus; that he is alive; that he is alive and powerful; that his revelation of the Father's dynamic love is just as true and just as available today as in the time when Jesus walked this earth. It is at heart the expectation that the covenant declaration, 'By his wounds you have been healed' is a promise on which we can stand and rely absolutely. Our faith, our expectancy, is not 'faith in our own faith', but faith in the Lord Jesus, who is alive for evermore and in whom alone there is salvation, deliverance and healing.

It is simple, uncluttered and child-like expectancy that gains heaven's response. This may sound unfair, but God requires of us a love relationship of trust, a walking hand-in-hand together with him throughout our lives. We are not to think of our heavenly Father as just a sort of emergency paramedic!

A major part of the expectancy we need to develop is our acceptance of his willingness to heal. When he asked the two blind men if they believed that he could heal them, their reply most obviously involved the belief that he was about to do it. He would hardly have thanked them politely for their trust and then left the house without reacting to their need!

> A man with leprosy came and knelt before him and said, "Lord, if you are willing, you can make me clean."
> Jesus reached out his hand and touched the man. "I am willing," he said. "Be clean!" Immediately he was cured of his leprosy.
>
> *Matthew 8:2,3*

This leper clearly knew that Jesus was capable of healing him, but his words suggest a hint of uncertainty about Jesus' willingness. The Lord's answer assures us all that being willing to heal is a constant, consistent, ongoing characteristic of God. Expectancy was present here, too.

We would do well to consider the rarity of healings in the church today in the light of Jesus' first recorded sermon to people in his home town, when they turned against him.

"I tell you the truth," he continued, "no prophet is accepted in his hometown. I assure you that there were many widows in Israel in Elijah's time, when the sky was shut for three and a half years and there was a severe famine throughout the land. Yet Elijah was not sent to any of them, but to a widow in Zarephath in the region of Sidon. And there were many in Israel with leprosy in the time of Elisha the prophet, yet not one of them was cleansed—only Naaman the Syrian."

All the people in the synagogue were furious when they heard this. They got up, drove him out of the town, and took him to the brow of the hill on which the town was built, in order to throw him down the cliff.

Luke 4:24–29

Jesus was teaching them why so many of God's children seem to miss out on the blessing of God. They needed to believe him—to believe his words to be true. Unbelief, lack of expectancy in Jesus' power and willingness to heal, issue in the rejection of Jesus as Messiah, and the people missing out on the blessing.

All the passages I quote underline the necessity for the three keys: expectancy, persistence and humility.

In the days of the prophet Elisha, as we read in II Kings 5, there lived in Syria a general called Naaman, commander of the army of the king of Syria, who led regular armed incursions into the northern kingdom of Israel. He was, indeed, a most valiant soldier, but, unhappily, he had leprosy. One of the raiding parties from Syria had taken captive a young girl from Israel, and she had become a servant to Naaman's wife. With surprising care, she said to her mistress, "If only my master would see the prophet who is in Samaria! He would cure him of his leprosy." Naaman, remarkably affected by the girl's expectancy, which he might so easily have dismissed with scepticism, went to the king of Syria and told him what she had said.

"By all means, go," the king of Syria replied. "I will send a letter to the king of Israel."

Naaman left, armed with his letter of introduction which read: 'With this letter I am sending my servant, Naaman, to you so that you may cure him of his leprosy.'

When the king of Israel read the letter from his enemy in Syria, he tore his robes in frustration and said, "Am I God? Can I kill and bring back to life? Why does this fellow send someone to me to be cured of his leprosy? See how he is trying to pick a quarrel with me!"

It looked as if it might have been a military trick. There was certainly not going to be a healing, as the king of Israel's expectancy appeared much smaller than a mustard seed! However, when Elisha heard that the king had torn his robes, he sent him this message: 'Why have you torn your robes? Have the man come to me and he will know that there is a prophet in Israel.'

So Naaman, still apparently filled with expectancy, and with a measure of persistence beginning to show through, left the royal court, went with his horses and chariots, and stopped at the door of Elisha's house. The general, so used to dealing with royalty, stooped to find himself at the door of an ordinary man. Testing Naaman's humility and persistence even further, Elisha sent a messenger out to say to him, "Go, wash yourself seven times in the Jordan, and your flesh will be restored and you will be cleansed."

At this point in the story, the general reached his threshold of patience and began to lose his humility altogether. "I thought that he would surely come out to me and stand and call on the name of the LORD his God, wave his hand over the spot and cure me of my leprosy. Are not Abana and Pharpar, the rivers of Damascus, better than any of the waters of Israel? Couldn't I wash in them and be cleansed?"

Naaman turned on his heel and went away in a rage. He had assumed that the healing would have been done in some suitable and appropriately ritualistic fashion; that the proper words would have been used and the proper form observed. Had he continued down that track he would most certainly not have been healed.

But still exercising their own expectancy and persistence, Naaman's servants went to him and said, "My father, if the prophet had told you to do some great thing, would you not have done it? How much more, then, when he tells you, 'Wash and be cleansed'!"

It is sometimes only a simple thing that God asks from us, and this may call for humility. There is no need for pomp and ceremony, no requirement for ritual, no proper words; he only asks for our expectancy, our persistence and our humility. But there was more demanded of Namaan. His persistence would be exercised further—no instant cure was there for him in the river; he had to do what he had been commanded to do. The one used to giving orders now had to obey. So Naaman went down and dipped himself in the Jordan seven times, as the man of God had instructed him. More humbling took place as he undressed beside the river in front of his men, revealing the full extent of what was seen as a frightening and disgusting disease. Down into the river he went: once, twice, three times. He would need persistence now. Nothing was happening. Up and down he went in front of his own men, allowing himself to look ridiculous as he dipped and stood in front of those he would command. Humility! Five, six, seven times, and only then he was healed.

Another miracle in the life of Elisha, recorded in II Kings 4:8ff, illustrates the same keys to releasing healing.

> The Shunammite woman said to her husband, "I know that this man [Elisha] who often comes our way is a holy man of God. Let's make a small room on the roof and put in it a bed and a table, a chair and a lamp for him. Then he can stay there whenever he comes to us."

They were doing a loft conversion in honour of a true man of God! One day, when Elisha came by that way, he went up to his room and lay down on the bed to rest awhile. He asked his servant, Gehazi, to call the Shunammite and when she arrived in the doorway he appreciatively asked her if they might speak on her behalf to the king or the commander of the army in thankfulness for all she had done for them. "I have a home among my own people," she replied.

Elisha wondered what could be done for her. Gehazi suggested to him that she had no son and that her husband was an old man, reducing the likelihood of her being adequately taken care of in her old age. "About this time next year," Elisha prophesied over her as she stood in the doorway, "you will hold a son in your arms."

"No, my lord," she objected. "Don't mislead your servant, O man of God!" She did not want her expectancy lifted in case her hopes were later to be dashed. Perhaps a son would be too much a miracle to hope for. How often do we hear such unbelief in the church today? So many have said that offering healing prayer is unfair as it might lift expectancy and then destroy faith if nothing happens. Here is the tragedy —expectancy is the very thing that needs to be lifted for the river of God to flow, and faith is rarely reduced by any apparent disappointment. The woman did indeed become pregnant, and the next year about that same time she gave birth to a son.

The child grew and prospered and one day ran out to his father who was working in the fields with the reapers. "My head! My head!" he complained to his father, who told a servant to carry the boy to his mother. The boy sat on her lap until midday, and then he died. Laying him on the prophet's bed, she shut the door behind her and went out to ask her husband to send her one of the servants and a donkey so that she could go quickly to the prophet, Elisha.

Even in the deepest of grief she had expectancy of God. "Why go to him today?" he asked. "It's not the New Moon or the Sabbath." Her persistence had set in, though. She was determined to go and find the prophet, so determined that she would not even tell her husband of the tragedy.

"It's all right," she said. Saddling the donkey, she told her servant not to slow down for her unless she told him to do so, and they set out to find the man of God at Mount Carmel. Whatever might happen on the way, she was filled with single-minded determination to get there.

Seeing her in the distance, Elisha became concerned and said to his servant, Gehazi, "Look! There's the Shunammite! Run to meet her and ask her, 'Are you all right? Is your husband all right? Is your child all right?'"

"Everything is all right," she said. Nothing was going to stop her reaching him now—her persistence was peaking. Dismounting in front of Elisha, in her humility, she lay down and took hold of his feet.

Gehazi came over to push her away, but Elisha said, "Leave her alone! She is in bitter distress, but the Lord has hidden it from me and has not told me why."

Now was the mourning mother's moment. "Did I ask you for a son, my lord?" she said. "Didn't I tell you, 'Don't raise my hopes'?"

Elisha, so keen to help and without hearing the rest of the mother's story, told Gehazi to tuck his cloak into his belt, take Elisha's staff in his hand and run. If he was to meet anyone, he was not to greet them, and if anyone greeted him, he was not to answer. Elisha then ordered him to lay the staff on the boy's face. But the child's mother said to Elisha, "As surely as the Lord lives and as you live, I will not leave you." So, in response to her persistence and expectancy, he got up and followed her. Elisha reached the house to find the boy lying dead on his couch. He went into the room, shut the door on the two of them and prayed to the Lord. Now it was his turn to be persistent. He got on the bed and lay on the boy, mouth to mouth, eyes to eyes, hands to hands. As he stretched himself out on the body, the boy became warm. For Elisha this contact with a dead human body would have been a totally defiling process —humility is almost too small a word for the act that God was requiring of him. Elisha had attempted a healing without total success, but some sign was there. Even more persistence was required of him. He turned away from the bed and walked back and forth in the room, then got on the bed and stretched out on the boy once more. Elisha's own persistence was coming into play. Eventually, the boy sneezed seven times and opened his eyes.

When the Shunammite woman came to see, Elisha said, "Take your son." Expectancy, persistence in soaking prayer, and humility before God had been necessary.

Now consider the account in the Acts of the Apostles, which describes Peter and John going up to the temple at the time of prayer—at three in the afternoon. At that very moment, a man who had been crippled from birth was being carried to the temple gate, where he was put every day so that he could beg from those going into the courts of the temple. Seeing Peter and John about to enter, he asked them for money. Peter said, "Look at us! Silver or gold I do not have, but what I have I give you. In the name of Jesus Christ of Nazareth, walk." Taking him by the right hand, he helped him up, and instantly the man's feet and ankles became strong.

Peter and John did not use any ritual—any particular words; they were not necessarily more anointed than many Christians today, but one thing is undeniable: they had *expectancy*. That expectancy must have been very great indeed for them to have taken him by the hand and helped him up. This action seems to indicate a readiness to persist until the ministry was complete. The helping up should not be seen as some sort of uncaring demonstration of blind self-assurance and triumphalist arrogance, but as something which could well have raised expectancy in the lame man himself. He would quickly have become aware that something had happened to him.

How sufferers' expectancy would have grown as they encountered Jesus; as they saw his actions, their faith would have grown stronger; as he put spittle on the blind man's eyes; as he told the cripple at Bethesda—and the man lowered down through the roof—to get up. Lepers were sent off to report their healing to the authorities before they had noticed a cure in themselves. In all these actions and words, sufferers begin to know that Jesus has authority and power and willingness to heal them; that something would be happening. Never let it be said that healing prayer is unfair as it raises expectancy! The raising of expectancy is good and right, as long as it is based on God's self-revelation in Jesus.

> They came to Bethsaida, and some people brought a blind man and begged Jesus to touch him. He took the blind man by the hand and led him outside the village. When he had spat on the man's eyes and put his hands on him, Jesus asked, "Do you see anything?"
>
> *Mark 8:22*

What expectancy was beginning to rise in the man's heart as Jesus ministered to him we cannot know, but we can imagine how it might have begun to rise up in him, as the Lord exercised his power and authority to heal in that gentle, firm and prolonged way.

On another occasion two blind men followed Jesus, calling out, "Have mercy on us, Son of David!" When Jesus had gone indoors, the blind men came to him, and he asked them, "Do you believe that I am able to do this?"

"Yes, Lord," they replied. His question would have established they really were in a place of expectancy. Then Jesus touched their eyes and told them that, according to their faith, it would be done to them.

When Paul went to Corinth, he did not go with eloquence or superior wisdom as he proclaimed the testimony about God. He went to them in weakness and fear, and with much trembling. His message and preaching were not with wise and persuasive words as so many of us might try to evangelize, but with a demonstration of the Spirit's power. In this way he trusted that their faith might not rest on men's wisdom, but on God's power. To the Romans he wrote that he would not speak of anything except what Christ had accomplished through him in leading the Gentiles to obey God by what he had said and done —with accompanying signs and miracles, through the power of the Holy Spirit. Moreover, he said that he had fully proclaimed the gospel of Christ. The full proclamation of the gospel must include the demonstration of signs and wonders or it will be considered by those hearing it to be just another available set of belief systems. And still there is great power available to those of us who believe.

I keep asking that the God of our Lord Jesus Christ, the glorious Father, may give you the Spirit of wisdom and revelation, so that you may know him better. I pray also that the eyes of your heart may be enlightened in order that you may know the hope to which he has called you, the riches of his glorious inheritance in the saints, and his incomparably great power for us who believe. That power is like the working of his mighty strength, which he exerted in Christ when he raised him from the dead and seated him at his right hand in the heavenly realms, far above all rule and authority, power and dominion, and every title that can be given, not only in the present age but also in the one to come. And God placed all things under his feet and appointed him to be head over everything for the church, which is his body, the fullness of him who fills everything in every way.

Ephesians 1:17–23

The power of God is moving amongst us even today. Every Christian, born again by the Spirit of God, baptised and filled with the same Holy Spirit, has in himself or herself the power of the new creation; the same power that raised Jesus from the dead. To affirm that truth is not arrogant; on the contrary, it is to acknowledge that all is by grace—the free gift of God. So as we raise the expectancy of sufferers by declaring, like the apostles, the power and authority of Jesus, and as we persist, and encourage others to persist, in proclaiming the gospel of salvation, we shall see more of heaven's 'dynamite'. The Greek word 'dunamis' means power, and our God has the power to heal now—today! Miracles happen!

What should our attitude be in all of this? —the attitude that would always cry out, "Have mercy on us, Son of David!"

We will see God move in power, but we need, at each moment, to be close to Jesus, walking in humble obedience to his words, for he said: "Whoever has my commands and obeys them, he is the one who loves me" (John 14:21).

8

A Measure of Faith

For by the grace given me I say to every one of you:
Do not think of yourself more highly than you ought,
but rather think of yourself with sober judgment, in
accordance with the measure of faith God has given
you. Just as each of us has one body with many
members, and these members do not all have the
same function, so in Christ we who are many form
one body, and each member belongs to all the
others.

Romans 12:3,4

Clearly, to be a Christian at all is to have faith. In John 1
we read that, '...to all who received him [Jesus] he gave
the right to become children of God.' This is saving
faith. Paul writes about faith in a different sense in the
Epistle to the Romans, when he speaks of a 'measure of
faith'. Our expectancy toward God, our depth of trust in

him to act in accordance with his covenant promises and his nature revealed in the Scriptures, will vary from believer to believer. Some have a strong expectation that God will act, whilst others struggle to believe it. God is unchanging; his nature is always the same; Christians seem to have different 'measures' of faith in what he will do. But note that Paul puts this in the context of the Body of Christ. The Christian whose expectancy is weak can be supported, upheld and encouraged by those who have stronger faith that God will act and move in power.

Consider the way faith (as expectancy) operates in some healing miracles. Sometimes, the faith of the supplicant is depicted as having a key part to play.

"You see the people crowding against you," his disciples answered, "and yet you can ask, 'Who touched me?'" But Jesus kept looking around to see who had done it. Then the woman, knowing what had happened to her, came and fell at his feet and, trembling with fear, told him the whole truth.

He said to her, "Daughter, your faith has healed you. Go in peace and be freed from your suffering."

Mark 5:31–34

There is no question here that there is any expectant faith involved other than that of the suffering woman. Neither the surrounding crowd nor Jesus himself have any idea that the miracle is happening until our Lord feels the healing power being released. Often, that is the order in which things happen at healing services and events. Someone comes to the venue with faith (expectation) that Jesus will heal them, and they may be touched and healed by him long before anyone 'ministers' to them. This should not surprise us, given that Gospel example.

In other miracles, all the expectancy comes from Jesus himself, as in those occasions when he raised people from the dead. When ministering for healing, we must never forget that it sometimes happens this way. God can heal without the sufferer having faith for his/her own healing. The faith (expectancy) in the person ministering can be used by God, and the miracle takes place. So if there seems to be nothing much happening, never allow any 'blame' to be placed upon a sufferer, even in thought, concerning their lack of faith (expectancy).

We also commonly see certain people healed of a particular illness who then seem to have a special anointing to heal others with the same disease. We must not make the mistake of thinking that having a sickness qualifies a Christian to heal it in others. The driving force here is that, knowing at first hand the wondrous grace of God in their own situation, their expectancy for healing in that one area is probably sky high —heaven opens, and their faith is answered by their seeing healing in others as they pray.

Expectant faith can also be corporate, arising in a gathering of believers. The expectancy of the supplicant, the minister, and other believers present can be added together in the heavenlies, by grace, to create something corporate. We are reminded of the promise in Matthew 18:19,

"If two of you on earth agree about anything you ask for, it will be done for you by my Father in heaven.

For where two or three come together in my name,
there am I with them."

Earlier in Matthew (8:23–26) Jesus had clearly taught
that his disciples' lack of faith was the root of a problem.
A sudden storm led them to cry out to him, and in their
fear they made the negative confession that they were
going to drown. Jesus' answer is most instructive:

He replied, "You of little faith, why are you so
afraid?" Then he got up and rebuked the winds and
the waves, and it was completely calm.

Evidently, they did not have enough faith expectancy
to quieten the storm.

But when there is corporate faith; when a sufferer is
brought by a group of men who clearly expected Jesus to
heal, their expectancy is richly rewarded:

A few days later, when Jesus again entered
Capernaum, the people heard that he had come
home. So many gathered that there was no room
left, not even outside the door, and he preached the
word to them. Some men came, bringing to him a
paralytic, carried by four of them. Since they could
not get him to Jesus because of the crowd, they
made an opening in the roof above Jesus and, after
digging through it, lowered the mat the paralyzed
man was lying on. When Jesus saw their faith, he
said to the paralytic, "Son, your sins are forgiven."

Mark 2:1–5

The man was healed and could pick up his mat and go home. The healing itself, however, took place at the moment when his sins were forgiven; and it is explicitly stated in the text that Jesus recognised their faith.

Present in any congregation are three kinds of faith expectancy: the minister's, the supplicant's and the congregation's as a corporate body. Although it is true that God sees us all as individuals, and is able to count even the hairs on our heads, he also sees a gathering of the Body of Christ as a corporate gathering, where all the faith can be added together to fire off an explosion of divine healing. In such settings, we who lead need to lift the expectancy of the congregation as a whole, in ways that are scriptural and in the context of Jesus-centred worship. God can use the faith-expectancy in the minister(s), in the people coming to receive healing, in those who have brought them, or in the praying, believing members of the congregation, or in any of these, and he releases miracles. Some situations seem to need more faith than others, and our trust levels can vary dramatically. Sometimes in the ministry of Christian healing, situations for which we might have insufficient faith have, in fact, pressed our trust and expectancy levels down below the ground, and we start from a negative position. From there, a greater degree of trust is required to push up above ground level, to the point where even mustard seed proportions are reached! By and large, life-threatening diseases seem to require the greatest boost of trusting expectancy; the medically incurable second, and those things that might be considered to be trifling, like the common cold or a headache, seem to us to be less challenging. But these are just our own perceptions. The truth, which we so often forget, is that nothing is too difficult for God. He wants his children to expect great things of him! He wants to see our faith! The Gospel accounts bear witness to this, as we have seen, and it is just as true in our meetings today. With him, all things are possible.

Negative thinking abounds, and we see how corrosive it can be in the healing ministry. Expressions overheard include:

"But, I'm not a Christian!"

"I'm over eighty."

"I tried it once before and nothing happened."

"Is that oil properly prepared?"

"My current lifestyle would probably not be approved of by the church."

"It's OK, I've learned to live with it."

"God put me on my back so that I could look up."

"I didn't really expect anything to happen but it was worth a shot."

"It may heal one day but it's all in God's timing!"

In the Gospel accounts of Jesus' healing ministry, such reservations and issues do not preclude the release of healing, though in the area of sin, the one who is healed will then be expected to turn from any wickedness. Healing may not always be preceded by repentance, but for the healed person to bear fruit they will often need to allow God to make other changes in their lives; they will need to give all the thanks and glory to Jesus who has healed them, or the healing will only be at the physical level.

So many of the quoted comments imply something

untrue, revealing negative expectancy, unbelief and complete misunderstanding of the revealed nature of God. Where in the Gospels do we see God putting a sickness on anyone? We see no such thing because his nature is to heal. Sickness is the work of the devil, not the work of God. Yet many Christians have a willingness to believe that sickness and pain may have redemptive qualities about them, and may even have been sent by God to offer redemptive opportunities. All these negatives, stemming from unbiblical teaching, are hindrances. The Holy Spirit leads us to Jesus, so that we can have a new love relationship with God as our Father in heaven as we receive Jesus as our personal Saviour and Lord of our life; and God's best plan and purpose for us is abundant life. Jesus said that he had come that we might have life and have it abundantly. Does that sound like a Saviour who would place sickness on people? Of course not!

Paul's 'thorn in the flesh' is often misguidedly cited as suggesting that God allows sickness for some redemptive purpose or other. An examination of the use of this expression, and others like it in the Old Testament, shows clearly that 'thorns in the flesh' are sometimes people, not necessarily illnesses. An example is to be found in the Book of Numbers 33:54–55.

Distribute the land by lot, according to your clans. To a larger group give a larger inheritance, and to a smaller group a smaller one. Whatever falls to them by lot will be theirs. Distribute it according to your ancestral tribes. But if you do not drive out the inhabitants of the land, those you allow to remain will become barbs in your eyes and thorns in your sides. They will give you trouble in the land where you will live.

Numbers 33:54–55

There is no biblical evidence to support the notion that illness can, in any way, be good for us. This is a teaching which developed in a later period.

In the Epistle of James, we read of tests and trials, but there is no suggestion that sickness comes from God:

James, a servant of God and of the Lord Jesus Christ, to the twelve tribes scattered among the nations: Greetings. Consider it pure joy, my brothers, whenever you face trials of many kinds, because you know that the testing of your faith develops perseverance. Perseverance must finish its work so that you may be mature and complete, not lacking anything.

James 1:1

Then, in James 5:14, we are given this guidance on the healing of sickness, underlining the truth that sickness is to be fought, not accepted as though it were from God:

Is any one of you sick? He should call the elders of the church to pray over him and anoint him with oil in the name of the Lord. And the prayer offered in faith will make the sick person well; the Lord will raise him up. If he has sinned, he will be forgiven.

Clearly, suffering as a result of persecution may result in benefits, but sickness certainly does not.

At this point, many of us who would love to be healed, but do not perhaps have the faith to ask for it or who have not yet received it, leap back into our own comfort zones by proclaiming something like, "Ah, but you must agree that God uses unhealed people so wonderfully!" — the inference being that God allows sickness to continue until he can get the best out of it. Somehow, we easily believe, in justification of an apparent lack of action on God's part, that his plans for us include our being ill, perhaps for the rest of our lives —but we will grin and bear it out of a sense of obedience, as it seems to serve his mysterious purposes. The next easy step from there is to reason that asking for healing displays lack of humility as it then seems to us that we would be praying against the will of God. This wholly mistaken attitude does not reflect the real nature of God revealed in Jesus. It is his nature to heal. Jesus never put sickness on anyone! Jesus never extended anyone's illness! He healed the sick who came to him or were brought to him.

Sickness is a disorder in God's creation and its source is sin (not necessarily that of the sufferer, of course), the disobedience of the world, and the devil —certainly not God. Believing that God is extending our illness gives us what we might call negative faith–expectancy: not faith for healing in Jesus' name but faith for a longer period of sickness; and that is a place where our healing can be even further delayed.

The truth is that our loving heavenly Father, who designed and created the universe, is by definition absolutely creative; he is our healer; he is not the author or extender of our sickness. Misunderstanding about this, if allowed to take root, can reduce our level of expectancy, and so have a devastating effect on our usefulness in the ministry of Christian healing.

One sign of a ministry team that really knows its business is to see one member defer to another when they themselves recognise their own lack of trust in a given situation. Such honesty is rare but precious.

A common, if often hidden evil is that of self-pity. This creeping malfunction of the soul pushes God out of the picture, despite all protestations to the contrary, and notwithstanding all the 'religious' activities of the person. New birth withdraws the central core of 'Me!' from the apple, replacing it with a new core which is Christ. Where previously there was only a sinful, self-centred human spirit, in the regenerated Christian the Holy Spirit has come and dwells within, where Jesus reigns as Lord and Saviour. The old, rotten core may have infected the surrounding flesh with its darkness, but that is the burden we should be seeking to shed on the walk to heaven's door. This life becomes the place where a process of sanctification begins. The old, putrid inner core is replaced with something godly when we receive Jesus. Self-pity is intensely damaging because it is a re-visiting of old attitudes which belong to the pre-conversion life; it is very far from the new walk of obedience to the Lord Jesus Christ, according to his word.

The fact is that the self-pitying person still has self firmly at the centre, rather than God. So those who come for prayer wanting only sympathy and a 'holy cuddle' may only receive that.

Giving up and even surrendering to a negative medical prognosis, is also unbelief. We need to begin to believe the truth that nothing is impossible for God. He even raises the dead!

> When Jesus entered the ruler's house and saw the flute players and the noisy crowd, he said, "Go away. The girl is not dead but asleep." But they laughed at him. After the crowd had been put outside, he went in and took the girl by the hand, and she got up.
>
> *Matthew 9:23–25*

The funeral rites were in full swing, the mourners and flute players engaged, and any suggestion that the girl could be raised up is laughed at. Such unbelief could block the healing movement of God and, knowing this full well, Jesus puts the unbelievers out of the room to effect the miracle. Peter ran into a similar situation in raising Dorcas from the dead, and needed to remove all those committed to the idea of death from the room.

> In Joppa there was a disciple named Tabitha (which, when translated, is Dorcas), who was always doing good and helping the poor. About that time she became sick and died, and her body was washed and placed in an upstairs room.
>
> Lydda was near Joppa; so when the disciples heard that Peter was in Lydda, they sent two men to him and urged him, "Please come at once!" Peter went with them, and when he arrived he was taken upstairs to the room. All the widows stood around him, crying and showing him the robes and other

clothing that Dorcas had made while she was still with them.

Peter sent them all out of the room; then he got down on his knees and prayed. Turning towards the dead woman, he said, "Tabitha, get up." She opened her eyes, and seeing Peter she sat up. He took her by the hand and helped her to her feet. Then he called the believers and the widows and presented her to them alive.

Acts 9:36–41

Unbelief had been removed from the situation to allow God's life-giving ministry to take place.

A service or meeting can comprise individuals with faith larger than a mustard seed, those with almost none at all, and those who (negatively) believe that God's healing grace is not for today or not for that moment. So should we attempt to discern any unbelief in ourselves and then remove ourselves and others from the meeting so as not to 'reduce the chances' of those who are earnestly seeking healing? At face value this would be in line with the actions taken both by Jesus and Peter when faced with unbelief, but we must be aware of what God wants to do in a situation, and be sensitive to the leading of the Holy Spirit. Often, Jesus' healing work would be a sign for unbelievers. Christian healing can work in that way. God's grace and mercy is much greater than we think, and we are to use the word of God to build faith, hope and expectancy; and, as we praise and worship the Lord and hear his word, faith can rise up in the hearts of those who are present. Faith comes from hearing God's word.

It may sometimes be appropriate to have a healing service in the local church, planned for those who would positively wish to be there. However, the finest way to see the corporate 'water table of expectancy' raised is to teach the Scriptures about healing in a simple and unsophisticated way, never emphasising all the failings of the church, but rejoicing with those who are healed, and revealing our heavenly Father's healing heart.

We must be ready to challenge such unworthy, negative, unbelieving thoughts as, "We might as well try it, there is nothing to lose!"

God wants to restore us and give us an abundant life, but we are prevented from receiving all that he has for us entirely by our lack of expectancy that he will do so.

9

Aspiring to Minister

Every minister within the church's healing ministry must
first and foremost be a disciple of the Lord Jesus Christ.
That discipleship must be maintained through prayer,
worship and the study of Scripture, the driving force
being a need to deepen a personal relationship with
God.

There is a reason for this attitude: the clean makes the
unclean clean. In Old Testament times, things were the
other way round. Walking on graves, contact with dead
bodies and many other things were seen as unclean, ne-
cessitating the process of ritual cleansing again and
again. With Jesus, it is different: the unclean is driven out
by the clean. We see this in such a physical act as touch-
ing a leper. Each minister of God's healing grace continues their own walk through life in the way of Jesus

Christ. In one sense this may often appear to be a way of weakness, yet, spiritually, it is the way that keeps us close to the source of true strength. In his humble obedience to the Father in all things, Jesus both *showed* the way and *is* the way, the truth and the life. Like Jesus, his Master, the minister of Christian healing does not rely upon human power but only on the Spirit of God. In this way of obedience and humility, it is essential that we find the right 'seat' at the 'wedding feast'.

> "When someone invites you to a wedding feast, do not take the place of honour, for a person more distinguished than you may have been invited. If so, the host who invited both of you will come and say to you, 'Give this man your seat.' Then, humiliated, you will have to take the least important place. But when you are invited, take the lowest place, so that when your host comes, he will say to you, 'Friend, move up to a better place.' Then you will be honoured in the presence of all your fellow guests."
>
> *Luke 14:8–10*

God has prepared a place in ministry for each longing heart which is for — and only for — him or her to fill. First of all, we come to his table, and ask that we might serve, looking even for the lowest tasks. When the work of service is done, then we may look for our own place at the table. We should not seek the most important place, in case it is reserved for someone else. The place that God has appointed is where we will be most content. A walk of obedience to the Father means having a submissive heart. Obedience to God is fundamental; without it, everything else is superficial. Obedience to those who have proper, biblical, God-given oversight and authority over us is important, too. Orthodox pastoral oversight is a precious gift that God gives his church, which is not to say that church leaders always get things right, nor that there is no need for processes of reform.

Accepting that fragments of selfish, fleshly or soulish impulses may still be at work in us can be the beginning of the wisdom that is needed by a disciple and minister. A teachable attitude is to be cultivated, and we must be ready to have fellowship and receive from mature Christian brothers and sisters who are walking closely with the Lord. Otherwise, we can all too easily become isolated and separated from the fellowship of believers.

A minister of healing needs to be ready to receive nurture, encouragement, teaching and, when necessary, correction. Churches, fellowships and ministries need structures that will help to make these things available.

As well as all this, essential to the growth of a minister of healing grace is that he or she knows the necessity of belonging to a tribe of 'Jabbok people'.

That night Jacob got up and took his two wives, his two maidservants and his eleven sons and crossed the ford of the Jabbok. After he had sent them across the stream, he sent over all his possessions. So Jacob was left alone, and a man wrestled with him till daybreak. When the man saw that he could not overpower him, he touched the socket of Jacob's hip so that his hip was wrenched as he wrestled with the man. Then the man said, "Let me go, for it is day-break."

But Jacob replied, "I will not let you go unless you bless me."

The man asked him, "What is your name?"

"Jacob," he answered.

Then the man said, "Your name will no longer be Jacob, but Israel, because you have struggled with God and with men and have overcome."

Gensis 32:22–28

Ministers in the field of pastoral care should fully recognise that, in the wrong circumstances and with the wrong influences, each one of us is capable of committing many kinds of sin. We, therefore, need to know the peace and acceptance of being in a secure home of intimacy with God, holding our own darkness to his light, before we are ever truly able to encourage others to go that way.

Therefore, I urge you, brothers, in view of God's mercy, to offer your bodies as living sacrifices, holy and pleasing to God—this is your spiritual act of worship. Do not conform any longer to the pattern of this world, but be transformed by the renewing of your mind. Then you will be able to test and approve what God's will is—his good, pleasing and perfect will. For by the grace given me I say to every one of you: Do not think of yourself more highly than you ought, but rather think of yourself with sober judgment, in accordance with the measure of faith God has given you.

Romans 12:1–3

Self-knowledge opens the door to humility and grace. Humility before God on the Christian's own personal 'island in the Jabbok river', and obedience, unlock blessing, and blessing is the provision of abundance — enough to fill our needs, to fulfil God's will for us, and to provide much to give to others. Many of us have spent a great deal of time seeking healing in our own lives, especially the wounds of the early years. We might imagine that healing results in God 'mending' us sufficiently for us to walk tall on our own two feet, but it is not so. The way to run the race is leaning on a staff! We do not receive healing gifts so that we may run on ahead and live on our own again, but so that we may be close to Jesus, by whose wounds we have been healed.

As we walk closely with him in the way of holiness, hanging on to his staff with both hands for dear life, our acknowledgement of weakness makes more and more room for his strength. His strength is actually made perfect in our own frailty. When people begin to minister to others, they often feel that they have to be strong in themselves, yet they experience many struggles, so the temptation is to become discouraged. The key is to go on praising; shouting alleluias to our precious Lord, and hanging on to his shepherd's crook .

Do not be anxious about anything, but in everything, by prayer and petition, with thanksgiving, present your requests to God. And the peace of God, which transcends all understanding, will guard your hearts and your minds in Christ Jesus.

Philippians 4:6–7

How often do our prayers consist only of, "Give me... give me... give me!" —interlaced, of course, with "Give them!" prayers? God is faithful and gracious, hearing and answering prayers, but how much better it is for us not only to come to him in times of trouble and need, but also to come to him simply to be in his company. Those of us who struggle with ourselves, and with the world, the flesh and the devil (in other words, all of us engaged in a real Christian walk of discipleship) know that close fellowship with Jesus, receiving from him, and constantly being filled with the Holy Spirit, is essential.

> Therefore, my dear friends, as you have always obeyed—not only in my presence, but now much more in my absence—continue to work out your salvation with fear and trembling, for it is God who works in you to will and to act according to his good purpose.
>
> *Philippians 2:12–13*

> Now to him who is able to do immeasurably more than all we ask or imagine, according to his power that is at work within us, to him be glory in the church and in Christ Jesus throughout all generations, for ever and ever! Amen.
>
> *Ephesians 3:20–21*

Walking in the Spirit means confronting the old nature and then learning to practise the presence of Jesus, learning to think a new way, living a new way, responding out of a new centre. It is a process that is learned and exercised; it does not find itself in a finished state at re-birth. For those of us who really do belong to Jesus there is going to be, at some point after conversion (and it may be many times), a confrontation with the Holy Spirit on a deeper and deeper level of the heart in which we find ourselves coming to the end of our own resources. We may do this again and then again, once more and once more again. Sanctification often looks like this. The moment of surrender to Jesus Christ marks the start of a battle against the self-centredness of the flesh which is at work in every human being. Most of us take up most of this time on earth plodding faithfully onwards, one step in front of the other, learning from our Lord as we go. A desert experience may form part of this. It makes no sense to imagine advancing into the heart of God at all without such periodic sojourns in places where we will be made to confront our own self-will, our demand to please self, our desire to go our own way. This is where the Holy Spirit brings us to the end of ourselves. There is a 'breaking' of everything in us which does not conform to the word of God, because God wants those who have been made holy by the blood of Jesus to learn and grow in holiness, day by day.

Every day, we have to face our own patches of inner darkness, our own inner struggles. We have to find our own place of solitude before the Lord, where he can deal with those things in the heart, just as surely as he has done with countless millions of other saints through the ages. In the faithful minister of healing, the Holy Spirit fosters sincerity, and trust in the wonderful, abiding presence of Jesus.

Now that same day two of them were going to a

village called Emmaus, about seven miles from
Jerusalem. They were talking with each other about
everything that had happened. As they talked and
discussed these things with each other, Jesus
himself came up and walked along with them....

Luke 24:13,15

Those who would heal the sick are a people called to live
on the Emmaus road —becoming aware of the living
presence of Jesus, and then leading others into his
presence. When others come to us searching for healing,
we, like Jesus, walk with them until that relationship is
marked by acceptance and trust. Then we allow the Holy
Spirit space for loving correction, conviction, re-thinking
and the recovery that follows. Jesus was prepared to
make friends with people who were marginalised in the
society of his day, and to risk being misunderstood in the
process. We are called to do the same, covering one
another in agapé love. The healing minister also has a
duty to God, who is providing all the gifts, as well as a
duty to those to whom ministry is offered, to ensure that
his or her spiritual hearing is acute.

Jesus said to him, "Away from me, Satan! For it is
written: 'Worship the Lord your God, and serve him
only.'" Then the devil left him, and angels came and
attended him.

Matthew 4:10–11

Jesus heard the Father's voice. He could distinguish it
perfectly from the deceptive voices of the world, the flesh
and the devil. We must learn to recognize the voice of

Jesus, and to obey what we hear, which is always in perfect conformity with the revealed word of the Bible. What we hear must be tested against the Scriptures because, although Jesus' sheep know his voice, our hearing is sometimes imperfect. We make mistakes. Sometimes that little 'voice' we think we hear can come out of our own inner compulsions! We are warned to take care that we only obey Jesus.

...And do not give the devil a foothold.

Ephesians 4:27

An 'inner voice' that seems of a compulsive nature — the little voice in one's head that keeps saying, 'You've got to do this,' or, 'You've got to do that' — may well not be from God. When God's Spirit speaks to our hearts, we are drawn to follow, but we are never pushed or driven.

...Where the Spirit of the Lord is, there is freedom.

II Corinthians 3:17b

God's way is not reflected in a driven, compulsive nature, and if we find that at work in ourselves, this is something that needs to be brought to the Lord so we can find that spiritual 'liberty' which is our inheritance as precious, forgiven, loved children of the heavenly Father.

How easy it is to fail to recognise our own ungodly behaviour and thought patterns; but when we acknowledge our wounds and sins, our compulsions and other character flaws, then we can bring them to Jesus, who is the light of the world. Each time that we come to the cross, acknowledging our sin and repenting, and receiving cleansing by the blood of Jesus, Satan loses one more foothold —and we begin to hear more clearly. The aim of the enemy in all this is to keep us in denial about our not-so-whole-and-holy areas. Being honest about our dark side, admitting our sins, faults, problems and weaknesses is always the first step in getting free from the enemy's deceit. Before we hold the light of Jesus to other people's darkness, we must learn to hold our darkness against his light.

A calling is not a compulsion but a gentle and loving longing of God. So, in the church's healing ministry, we are asked to be God-centred, emptying ourselves of pride, self seeking and anything which would intrude ourselves into the healing situation. It is the Lord Jesus Christ who heals. We are not 'healers' in our own name and power; we are those who respond to his command to 'heal the sick' —but only in his precious name, relying on his power alone, and giving him all the glory. Personal power-seeking and self-glorification, which are so destructive, are utterly foreign to this commission from the Lord to his church.

The life to which the Christian aspires, if he or she is to see the glory of God in mighty acts of salvation, healing and deliverance in the lives of others, means being ready to declare and speak boldly and with confidence the wonderful scriptural promises; and also having the humility to let the river flow, as the Holy Spirit moves. The reward is in knowing that we do the will of our Lord Jesus; and then, daily, we also have the most extraordinary thrill of seeing the results of expectant faith and the anointing of God!